Bead Crochet Snakes
History and Technique

ADELE ROGERS RECKLIES

Reckless Beading Press
Brooklyn, NY 11215

Beaded Crochet Snakes: History and Technique
Text © 2005, Adele Rogers Recklies
Photos © 2005, Don Recklies
Illustrations © 2005, Don Recklies

Published by Reckless Beading Press
420 4th Ave. #1
Brooklyn, NY 11215
www.beadcrochetsnakes.com

Editor: Jean Campbell
Technical Editor: Bonnie Brooks
Cover and interior design: 1106 Design, LLC
Illustrations and charts: Don Recklies
Photos: unless specified, all photos by Don Recklies

Library of Congress Cataloging-in-Publication Data:

Recklies, Adele

Bead Crochet Snakes: History and Technique/Adele Rogers Recklies, author; photographs by Don Recklies-1st ed.

p.cm.

ISBN: 978-0-9791649-0-3 (soft cover)

1. Beadwork 2. Handicraft 3. World War 1914-1918 I. Title

Library of Congress Control Number 2006938942

Printed in the United States of America by Bookmasters

CONTENTS

ACKNOWLEDGMENTS

I would like to offer my heartfelt thanks and gratitude to the following people who helped to make this book a reality:

My mother, who patiently taught a little left-handed girl to knit and started me on my life-long love of both needlework and books.

Miriam Milgram, who taught me to bead crochet and has enthusiastically shared her knowledge of Balkan beadwork.

Lydia Borin and Suzanne Cooper for their encouragement and advice throughout the process.

The late Joan Dworkin, who sold me my first Turkish POW snake and, with her husband Frank, showed me how much fun beadwork collecting could be. Rest in peace, Joan.

Jane Kimball, trench art expert extraordinaire, fellow collector, and research buddy.

My pattern testers: Yoshie Marubashi, Anne Phillips, Michele Kopack, and my February 2006 Bead Crochet Snake Bracelet class.

In Turkey, Sadik Sagiroglu and Riza Sekerci, who translated Turkish phrases and provided information on modern prisoner beadwork.

Yvonne Cresswell, Manx National Heritage, who provided further information on the Knockaloe Camp snakes given to local families.

Stefany Tomalin, for alerting me to the bead crochet snake pattern in Leach's Beadwork and the Bead Society of Great Britain for allowing me to reprint the photo from their newsletter.

And, most importantly Don, my dear husband of more years than I care to admit, who has always been willing to help with the technical details of any project and never flinches when he hears me ask for "just one more chart."

Why is Everybody Always Picking on Me?, Adele Rogers Recklies, 2005, 15' 6" (4.8 m) long.

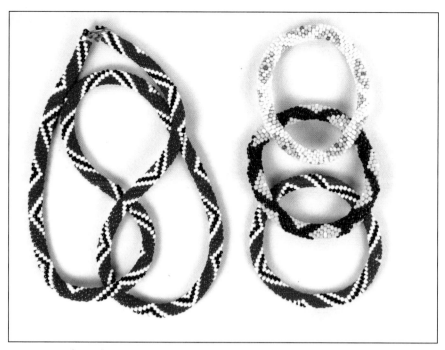

A necklace and three bracelets made by the author from traditional Balkan patterns gathered by Miriam Milgram and shared with the Balkan bead crochet class.

INTRODUCTION

This book grew out of a class entitled "Balkan Tubular Bead Crochet" that I innocently attended in early 1997. I took to the technique right away and, despite my fear of real snakes, sorely wanted to make a beadwork snake similar to the one the instructor had showed us. When it became apparent that a beaded snake class would not be offered, I set about researching bead crochet snakes in order to make my own decorative reptile. Little did I know I would still be delving into this fascinating subject for many years.

I was immediately dismayed to find almost no information, at least in English, on any kind of bead crochet snake, neither those made by villagers in Southeastern Europe that were similar to what I had seen in that class nor those made by World War I prisoners-of-war. Finding one small photo as inspiration, I came up with a pattern for a beaded snake that could not only decorate

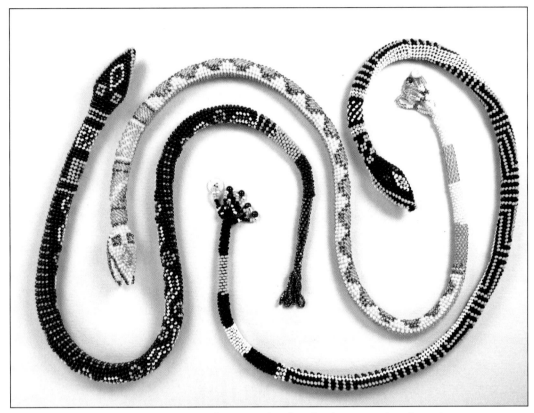

Three snakes by Miriam Milgram that inspired my own bead crochet snake journey. Each snake measures about 23″ (58.5 cm).

a table but could be worn as a necklace. That led to a rattlesnake necklace pattern, two versions of a snake bracelet, a snake bracelet with memory that wraps around a wrist, and a fifteen foot, six inch snake with writing all along the belly. What started as a three-page instruction sheet for my first snake necklace has now grown into a book that includes patterns as well as a history of bead crochet snakes.

The research into antique bead crochet snakes and other items has been exciting and frustrating at the same time. Exciting because I have discovered many beautiful and intricately beaded objects, frustrating because most items come up for sale with no accompanying oral or written records. While the snakes were important items to the people who owned them, subsequent generations saw no value in the snakes and rarely asked questions about their origins. For example, I bought five beaded items that had belonged to the seller's grandmother in Swansea, United Kingdom: one bead crochet snake dated 1917, one smaller bead crochet snake, one loomed choker that said "TURKISH PRISONERS" on it, and two bead crochet ropes that looked like small necklaces. The objects (shown on the next page) were clearly treasured by their original owner but no one had asked Grandma how she had acquired the items. Since the seller said that no one in the family had served in World

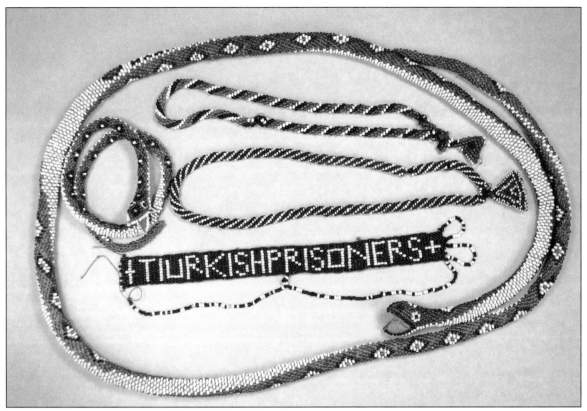

Turkish prisoner-of-war beadwork from World War I owned by a woman in Swansea, United Kingdom.

War I and brought the beadwork back as souvenirs, we are left to speculate how and why these items ended up in the woman's possession. Did she buy them during World War I to support men interned in Great Britain? Were they a gift? Did she buy them later in her life? Did she travel to Turkey and buy them there? We will never know.

We *do* know that the story of beadwork snakes and other souvenirs is not only that of Turkey, but encompasses some of the other countries that made up the Ottoman Empire in the last quarter of the eighteen hundreds. Perhaps influenced by the nineteenth-century fashion for European culture, bead crochet was practiced in parts of Turkey, Greece,

Bulgaria, Albania, Macedonia, Syria, Palestine, Iraq, and even Algeria. Civilian prisoners throughout the Ottoman Empire were making small craft items to pass time or raise extra money even before World War I and bead crochet was one of the techniques employed. The prisoner-of-war snakes and other trinkets were part of a handwork tradition that continues even today.

Although many of the snakes say "TURKISH PRISONER OF WAR" on the individual bellies, their makers may not have all been strictly Turkish. Members of the Central Powers' military and interned civilians held in all British camps in 1917 included Germans, Austrians, Turks, Bulgarians, Armenians, Greeks, Jews from

Palestine and Mesopotamia, Egyptians, Arabs, and Bedouins. Many of these men may have already been familiar with bead crochet from watching their wives, sisters, or sweethearts practice the popular craft. It wouldn't be much of a stretch for such men to take up bead crochet themselves.

Regardless of the exact nationality of the prisoners making the beaded souvenirs of World War I, the surviving snakes still fascinate us; even those who have no desire or skill to make a similar snake wonder about their origins. My goal is to both provide answers to some common questions and to show the variety of bead crochet snakes that were crafted beyond the prison camps of World War I. Whether a souvenir, engagement present, form of sympathetic magic, or simple adornment, bead crochet snakes come in a variety of forms and patterns.

For those who want to try their hand at crocheting a snake, I have included five of my own patterns for beaded snake necklaces and bracelets that are suitable for those who bead crochet at an intermediate or advanced level. If you are a bit apprehensive at working with such small beads, you can try one of the smaller snakes with size 8° beads, size 10 crochet thread and a steel hook somewhere around a size 6 (1.80 mm). Once you are familiar with the process, you can move down to size 10° or 12° beads for the next one. I say next one because once you try a bead crochet snake, you may find yourself hooked on them. I hope that my patterns will inspire you to come up with your own designs, continuing a tradition that spans almost a century.

Photo 1. Three antique bead crochet belts from Bulgaria.

HISTORY

The story of bead crochet snakes is a rich one that involves a geographical area formerly referred to as the Balkans and known today as Southeastern Europe. Within that region, bead crochet items were mostly produced in Albania, Bulgaria, Greece, the Republic of Macedonia, and eastern Turkey.

The history of these intriguing objects also involves the Ottoman Empire, which, at its height, controlled Anatolia, the Middle East, parts of North Africa, and much of Southeastern Europe. Ottoman influence can be seen in the flowering of textiles and needlework, the tradition of handicrafts in prison, and, perhaps, some of the widespread belief in snakes as good luck symbols.

The majority of beadwork reptiles made in the region can be divided into three types: snakes and lizards made by Turkish soldiers imprisoned in British military and civilian internment camps during World

War I, snakes made by villagers in parts of Southeastern Europe for their own use, and less elaborate snakes made to be sold at markets as souvenirs or made specifically as jewelry.

While the snakes made by imprisoned soldiers and civilians during World War I are the most well-known items of bead crochet, the story of their making actually encompasses an interest in needlework, the use of crafts as a way to keep busy or make money in prison, the veneration of snakes, and their use in real life or art as protection against misfortune. The story starts with the practice of crochet in the Ottoman Empire.

CROCHET IN THE OTTOMAN EMPIRE

While people have some familiarity with the beaded snakes made by Turkish prisoners of war during World War I, the colorful serpents are actually part of a tradition of crochet, with or without beads, popular in parts of the Ottoman Empire. Many needlework historians even believe that crochet developed in the same area from tambouring, a form of embroidery that employs a fine hook that was practiced in Turkey, Persia, and India before it reached Europe in the seventeen hundreds.

Although there may not be conclusive evidence that crochet originated

Photo 2. A wooden bottle with a bead crochet cover, approximately 9" (23 cm) high. The date 1893 is worked in beads on the bottom of the bottle.

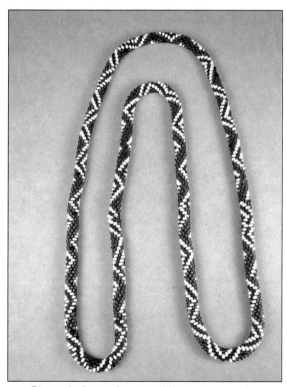

Photo 3. An antique necklace, measuring 37" (94 cm) in length, that employs a traditional zig-zag pattern.

in Turkey, there are indications that some form of the craft was well established in the country by 1878, when Fanny Blunt described the activities of shopkeeper's daughters: "Embroidery, indispensable in a number of useless articles that serve to figure in the *trousseau* of every Turkish girl, and latterly coarse needle and crochet-work, fill up part of the time, while the mothers attend to their household affairs....In the capital, however, less of this kind of employment is indulged in by the fashionable *hanoum*, who are trying to create a taste for European occupations by learning music, foreign languages, and fine needlework."[1]

Despite the reference to coarse crochet-work that was earlier employed to make socks, women were certainly doing fine crochet work with beads in the Ottoman Empire by the end of the nineteenth century. Women's folk dress in parts of Thrace and Bulgaria included flat, bead crochet belts like the three shown in Photo 1 while corresponding men's costumes included bead crochet pocket watch holders like the ones in Photo 7. The Bulgarian man in Photo 9 sports such a pocket watch holder in the right-hand pocket of his vest. Bottles, both wooden and glass, were decorated with colorful bead crochet covers; one such wooden bottle, shown in Photo 2, can be easily dated by the "1893" worked in beads on the bottom. Crochet with fine thread and beads also became one of the techniques used in the nineteenth and twentieth centuries to make the decorative edging called oya found on scarves, clothing, and textiles like napkins, tablecloths, and bedcovers. Two

Photo 4. Two contemporary examples of Turkish scarves decorated with oya; the *top* green one is crocheted with thread and beads while the *bottom* orange one is crocheted with just thread.

modern examples of oya on scarves can be seen in Photo 4.

Continuing into the twentieth century, women in parts of Bulgaria, Macedonia, Greece, and Turkey also used the bead crochet technique to fashion tubes that were worn as bracelets, necklaces like the one in Photo 3, and lengths of beaded tubes that draped across the chest or hung from belts. Enlargement of the bead crochet tubes resulted in triangular ornaments, rosaries made of beaded beads or egg-shaped pendants like those in Photo 6. Further enlargement of the beaded tubes formed coin purses like those in Photo 5 and snakes of all sizes. Aside from adornment, bead crochet items also served as protection

Photo 5. *Top,* Greek bead crochet coin purse, dated 1900, measuring 3" x 3" (7.5 cm x 7.5 cm); *bottom,* a fragment of a miser's purse from Bulgaria, dated 1912.

against the evil eye, illness, or misfortune in general.

While bead crochet was done mostly by women, men sometimes made items while incarcerated in prison to sell for money, give as gifts, or send to family members. Turkish soldiers even made a few beadwork souvenirs, mainly small coin purses, like the two seen in Photo 8, during their leisure time.

Photo 6. *Left,* bead crochet egg-shaped pendant on a bead crochet rope, date unknown; *right,* Turkish Muslim rosary, made of 33 bead crochet beads, ca. 1925, and measuring 25" (63.5) long including decoration.

Photo 7. Three bead crochet pocket watch holders, early twentieth century, the largest is 8½" (21.5 cm) long.

Photo 8. Two bead crochet purses, possibly made by Turkish soldiers, dated 1954 and 1952. *Top,* 4" x 2½" (10 cm x 7.5 cm), *bottom,* 4" x 3" (10 cm x 7.5 cm).

Photo 9. Photo showing a man from Chokoba, Rhodopi area wearing traditional Bulgarian dress, ca. 1880s. Note the long section of a beadwork pocket watch holder similar to those in Photo 7 dangling from the vest pocket on the left. *Left,* detail of the long section of the pocket watch holder.

HANDICRAFTS IN PRISON

The tradition of making craft items in prison to raise a little money or pass the time goes back to at least the nineteenth century in parts of the former Ottoman Empire. Although she doesn't mention beadwork specifically, Maude Parkinson describes such activities in a prison in Ocna Mare, Romania: "They [the prisoners] are allowed to manufacture small articles of salt, wood, etc. and stalls are arranged in the courtyard of the prison on which these articles are exposed for sale, the prisoners themselves acting as salesmen."[2] She also tells of attending an exhibition in Bucharest that included examples of prisoners' work as part of a larger exhibit showing the improvement in treatment of incarcerated persons compared to former times. Burton Holmes wrote of traveling in nineteenth-century Morocco, where Tangier prisoners eked out an existence by begging or making and selling colored baskets. He noted that "The presence of a traveler becoming known in the den, baskets by the dozen came tumbling out [of an aperture] to tempt him in charity to buy."[3]

Examples of prison beadwork can be found in various museums. Marischal Museum in Aberdeen, Scotland has two

Photo 10. Three bead crochet items made by civilian prisoners in Turkey. *Left,* cigarette lighter cover probably from the 1950s; *right,* two contemporary key chains. The largest key chain is 2" x 9" (5 cm x 23 cm).

crochet and beadwork drawstring purses made by prisoners in Albania that were collected by Margaret Hasluck before she was forced to leave the country by the hostilities of World War II.

Miriam Milgram noted that the Historical Museum of Blagoevgrad, Bulgaria owns a beaded chain with a snake's head that was made by a Bulgarian priest in Thessalonika while serving a sentence for political activity. She also observed that the Gotse Delcheve History Museum, Bulgaria has a beaded bottle cover and purse made by a Macedonian revolutionary in 1910 while he was imprisoned on the island of Rhodes.[4]

Some of the artifacts made by Hungarian prisoners in the nineteenth and twentieth centuries were even gathered together for an exhibit in 2001 entitled Art Under Pressure. The items exhibited included a wooden guitar, textiles, paintings, woodcarvings, and a beadwork-covered bottle and drinking glass holder.[5]

Beadwork items were also made by people incarcerated in Turkey, Egypt, Syria and Iraq. In Iraq, the practice continued as late as Sadam Hussein's reign. One prisoner, Salam Al-Magsosi employed a two-stranded form of bead crochet to make items that he would give to the guards in exchange for food and cigarettes while imprisoned in Iraq. He is currently living in the United States and continues to make purses, necklaces, coasters, and vases out of beads and thread.[6] Egyptian prisoners make beadwork bags, purses, key chains, jewelry, and pens to help pay their living

Photo 11. Two contemporary bead crochet small purses made by civilian prisoners in Turkey. Both purses measure about 5″ x 4″ (13 cm x 10 cm) and are lined with velvet.

expenses. Some of the beadwork items are sold in the United Kingdom or over the internet by the Christian Prisoners Support Network.

In Turkey, the tradition of making beaded items in prison started as a way to keep busy and make gifts for loved ones on the outside. Prisoners asked their visitors for the required glass beads, although after the 1950s beads were also sold in the prison canteens or cafeterias.

There are currently three prisons in Turkey where simple items like key chains, cigarette lighter holders, necklaces, and small purses are still being made. Collectors can sometimes buy items directly from prison officers, but a few dealers buy beadwork pieces in bulk from the prisons. These items are then sold to small businesses, like magazine booths, which sell the beadwork to the public. Though the number of such booths and shacks selling prisoner beadwork is now decreasing throughout Turkey, contemporary and vintage purses, key chains, cigarette lighter covers, ornaments that hang in doorways or cars, Muslim rosaries, and necklaces show up for sale on Ebay on a fairly regular basis.[7] Example of such souvenirs can be seen in Photos 10–13. Unfortunately,

Photo 12. Three bead crochet items made by civilian prisoners in Turkey. *Top and Bottom,* beadwork loops with pendants that serve as Muslim rosaries, worry beads, or automobile ornaments, the largest measuring 10″ (25.5 cm) in length; *middle,* necklace measuring 15″ (38 cm) with matching bracelet.

I have yet to find a prisoner-made bead crochet snake among the contemporary items for sale.

SNAKE FOLKLORE OF THE REGION

The question might spring to mind as to why people throughout Southeastern Europe made bead crochet snakes instead of other animals common to the area? Aside from the practical fact that a snake is mostly a tube with one wide end for the head, the answer may be found in the folklore of the region. Many rural populations considered snakes to be good luck, a practice commented upon in more than a few travelogues written at the end of the nineteenth century.

One such travel account observed that "The Vlach women of European Turkey, who inhabit villages in the mountain ranges of Thessaly and Albania, treat serpents with a great respect and even with Veneration. If one of the harmless white snakes which abound in the country chances to enter a cottage, it is provided with food and allowed to depart unharmed, its appearance indoors being accounted a lucky event. Such friendly treatment often results in the snake's becoming domesticated and receiving the title of "house-serpent."[8]

Snakes were also welcomed into houses in parts of Turkey, Bulgaria, Russia, and Romania. The image of a snake often decorated the distinctive gates in front of Romanian homes as "the symbol of perseverance in a country where many houses are believed to have a snake which is never seen but none the less protects the home."[9] Even today Turkey's

Photo 13. Loom-work, fringe, and bead crochet ornament with two free-swinging birds, 3" x 6" (7.5 cm x 15 cm). The ornaments are often, but not always, made by civilian prisoners in Turkey. Arabic in origin, Masallah can be translated as "May God preserve from evil."

Ministry of Culture and Tourism website includes the popular belief that "A snake in the house, guards it."[10]

Outside of the home, snakes were venerated in other ways. In Orman, Yugoslavia the villagers would participate in a snake festival as part of the celebration of the Feast of the Forty Martyrs in the spring. Hibernating snakes were gathered and place at the crossroads where musicians played on drums and flutes to wake the snakes while the women danced in a ring. Everyone dropped handkerchiefs, scarves, stockings, belts and the like on the road in the hope that the snakes would crawl over the clothing three times and grant a wish or give fertility.[11]

Such respect for snakes was not always beneficial to the animal in question. Edith Durham described an amulet used in parts of the Balkans against the evil eye that was made up of a dried snake's head enclosed between two silver St. George's [coins] and blessed by the priest.[12] In nineteenth-century Turkey, superstition required that vipers should be used medicinally in the spring, so the gypsies collected live snakes and sold them to townspeople. In Estonia, it was believed that a snake killed before St. George's Day had magic powers even if it was later used in a dried form, made into a powder, ashes, or infused in oil or spirits.

Given that serpents were held in such high regard, bead crochet snakes could be seen as a form of sympathetic magic similar to carving the likeness into a wood post or a good luck amulet that was more easily obtained than killing a live snake and cutting off its head.

SNAKE AND DRAGON FOLKLORE

Along with the beaded snakes, Turkish prisoners of war produced bead crochet animals that are described as lizards by collectors. Taking into consideration the regional belief that a dragon was a form of snake, the beadwork lizards may instead be representations of a dragon. The two animals are certainly connected in the instances where Turkish prisoners made bead crochet lizards that were caught in the mouths of bead crochet snakes.

The snake folklore found in Southeastern Europe intertwines with the superstition and myth that revolves around St. George and the dragon, which is seen by many as nothing more than a large, winged snake. Olive Lodge noted this connection when she observed in 1944 that "Many spring songs, sung on St. George's Day, chant of fertility and harvest, the green things of the earth, shepherds and flowers, snakes and dragons...The dragon, of course, is a great snake."[13] In Estonia, more than one-tenth of the reports concerning St. George's Day customs have something to do with snakes. Two of the examples of snake veneration mentioned in the previous section also involve St. George.

In Turkey, a dragon is believed to derive from a snake. In the mythology of the Turcik people of northern and central Eurasia, the dragon is embodied as a snake or lizard and is a symbol of power. In Turkey, the mythical figure of the dragon is seen as deriving from the snake and both animals show up in the artwork of Turkey. To give one example, weavers in the important carpet center of Ladik in Anatolia count snakes and dragons among the symbols for luck and prosperity woven into their carpets. Like the use of beadwork snakes as sympathetic magic, the production of bead crochet dragons in the form of lizards by World War I prisoners of war may have served the same purpose.

Photo 14. An example of a Turkish prisoner-of-war snake
with writing on the top side of the body.

PRISONER-OF-WAR SNAKES

While there may have been a few bead crochet snakes made before World War I, this form of folk art blossomed during the imprisonment of enemy soldiers and civilians caught up in the Great War and the lengthy repatriation of internees afterwards. The two centers of production were the internment camps in Great Britain, notably Knockaloe Camp on the Isle of Man, and the prisoner-of-war camps setup by Britain in Egypt and Cyprus. A few snakes have been found with documentation that indicates an origin in Salonika, Cyprus, and even France but the majority of snakes and lizards made during captivity came from Egypt and England.

Unfortunately, documentation pertaining to the craft programs in internment camps is spotty owing to destruction of official World War I records during subsequent wars and Turkey's aggressive modernization. Luckily, remaining reports, written accounts by charity workers in the camps, oral histories from the inhabitants of the Isle of Man, and memoirs of individual snake owners give us a picture of the circumstances surrounding the bead crochet reptiles and their journey into the world beyond the barbed wire.

Craft programs and other means to occupy time were needed to combat the despondency fostered by large numbers of men held in close quarters for extended periods of time. In 1914, over 23,000 men were interned as prisoners of war in various parts of the United Kingdom. By 1916 that number had climbed to 38,384 military, naval, and civilian prisoners in twenty-three detention camps throughout Great Britain. Despite the end of fighting on November 11, 1918, there were still 1,500 men awaiting release from Knockaloe Camp as of June 30, 1919.

The number of interned soldiers in Egypt who had to be kept occupied was even greater than those imprisoned in England. Toward the end of the war, two of the major prison camps, Heliopolis and Bilbeis, each held more men than were confined in all of England. Crafts such as beadwork, may not have only been a way to pass time or make a bit

Photo 15. Turkish bead crochet, prisoner-of-war snake showing a typical zig-zag pattern, measuring 67" (170 cm). The belly sports the misspelled phrase "TURKISH PHISONERS 1918."

of money, but may have also offered a way to inject a small amount of beauty or a reminder of home into harsh circumstances.

In Egypt the organization of leisure activities such as the crafts program for captured soldiers seems to have been placed under the authority of the British military, although there were certainly workers from charitable organizations visiting the prisoner-of-war camps. Supplies for leisure activities were provided by the military and finished beadwork was somehow sold in local curiosity shops.

In England, the same charitable organizations that offered relief in Egypt played a major part in organizing the craft programs for the internees, providing buildings to serve as workshops, and arranging for the sale of completed craft items. Materials for craft programs

Photo 16. Small bead crochet Turkish prisoner-of-war snake with a diamond pattern, measuring 21″ (53.5 cm).

were provided by donations of supplies themselves or money. While the idea for a crafts program is reported to have started with a few sailors making models and ornaments on their own to pass the time, the program soon grew into something resembling "Big Business."

There is no proof of any sharing of instructions between craft programs in Egypt and England, but the fact is that the bead crochet snakes made in both countries are so similar in style that there is currently no way to tell them apart without accompanying documentation. Leaving aside tantalizing speculation, there is enough information about the internee craft programs in Great Britain to give us an idea of prisoner-of-war activities in both countries.

BEADED SNAKES AND OTHER CRAFTS IN ENGLAND

Captured soldiers and civilian internees held in detention camps throughout Great Britain produced beadwork and other craft items as part of recreation programs set up by relief organizations to fight the stress of prolonged confinement and separation from families. As a breezy subaltern stationed at Knockaloe Camp explained to Mr. George Leach of the *Manchester Guardian* in October, 1916, "You must either give 'em something to do or let them go 'dotty'."[14] Charitable organizations, including the Society of Friends, the American Young Men's Christian Association, and the German Red Cross Society, worked with the authorities to make the confinement

Photo 17. Two examples of World War I, Turkish POW beadwork. *Top,* purse with loomed top, netted body, and strung handle, measuring 5" x 14" (12.5 cm x 35.5 cm). The loomed portion says "TURKISH 19 PRISONERS 19." *Bottom,* a loomed choker, measuring 1" x 12" (2.5 cm x 30.5 cm). Part of the left-side beading and half of the fastener have been lost.

more bearable by providing the prisoners with means to occupy their time. The relief organizations also worked with their counterparts in Germany to assure fair treatment of British soldiers in German prison camps.

In England, the main body entrusted with organizing the "handicraft occupations" was the Emergency Committee for the Assistance of Germans, Austrians, and Hungarians in Distress formed by the Society of Friends. While the committee was originally organized to give general help to interned men who had been living in Great Britain, as well as their families left behind, the crafts program eventually proved to be a major method of offering emotional and financial relief to a growing number of prisoners.

Throughout the war the Emergency Committee managed to start craft programs for men in most of the camps located in Great Britain as well as actively solicit and collect donations of money, materials for craft work, books, games, musical instruments, tools, and garden seeds for the prisoners. They also imposed quality standards for items put up for sale and kept a design library of "models" from which men could work. The committee, working with the Y.M.C.A. War Prisoners Aid, also arranged the sale of thousands of articles made in detention camps and large working parties.

Owing to War Office regulations, though, committees made up of the internees themselves had to organize most of the craft and educational activities for each camp. Often experts in different crafts who could pass on their skills were found among the prisoners in the various camps, though occasionally teachers from outside were allowed into the camps.

Prisoners throughout camps in Great Britain managed to produce a staggering variety of small items. The beadwork souvenirs included the bead crochet snakes from Knockaloe Camp and necklaces made of paper beads. Other items made by the detainees include carved and inlaid boxes and picture frames, dainty little animals made from

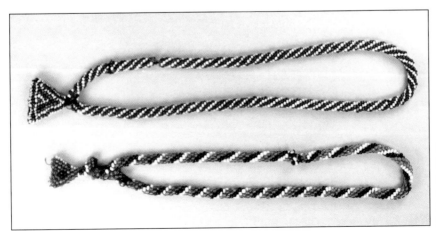

Photo 18. Two World War I, Turkish prisoner-of-war Muslim rosaries or worry beads. These items are well used and have been repaired.

cuttlefish molds filled with melted "silver-paper" collected by British children, wooden animals with jointed limbs, toys, inlaid match cases, chess sets, letter openers, boxes, intricate wood carvings, model ships in bottles, mechanical models, and carved bone vases, brooches, and napkin rings.

The majority of the craft items were produced at the Knockaloe Camp on the Isle of Man. By virtue of its size, concentration of poor men, and isolated location, Knockaloe Camp occupied much of the Emergency Committee's time and effort. Holding over 23,000 men divided into four individual camps by the end of the war, Knockaloe was large enough to eventually merit five full-time Friends' workers on the island. One of the most active workers was James Baily, an expert handicraft teacher whose role started as Camp Visitor helping with handwork occupation and ended up as the governmental Industrial Superintendent of all the work performed by the interned men in the Knockaloe Camp.

So many Friends were needed on the island because Knockaloe Camp produced more than just small decorative items. On a larger scale, workshops

Photo 19. Turkish prisoner-of-war snake with zig-zag pattern, dated 1919, measuring 65" (165 cm).

were set up in the camp for woodworking and furniture making, studios for fine artists, corners for jewelers and metalworkers, and spaces for leatherwork, raffia, and basket making. There was also a bookbinders' shop, lithography or steel engraving press, looms for woven stuffs, and a room full of knitting machines to make new socks for the prisoners themselves.

By 1915 the prisoners' increasing stream of requests for craft materials and tools led the Friends Emergency Committee to set up their own hut among the official storehouses just outside the main entrance to the camp. Each morning

representatives of the Industrial Committees from each of the four camps plus their guards arrived at the store to turn over completed items for sale and load their hand trucks with newly arrived craft materials.

The few specific references to beadwork snakes made in Great Britain all speak of snakes made on the Isle of Man. Recounting details of the Knockaloe internment camp, Frank C. Quayle of Peel wrote that "Turkish prisoners with a detailed knowledge of wild life in their native land, produced a great variety of beaded snakes; the open mouth of the snakes were used as pin cushions and

Photo 20. Turkish prisoner-of-war snake with diamond pattern, dated 1917, measuring 60″ (152.5 cm).

the body of the reptile was slung over the shoulder so enabling the sewer to work freely with both hands. So realistic were these snakes in execution and colouring that I have seen people back away from them as if they were alive."[15] Given that no other reference has been found to the use of the snakes as pin cushions, it doesn't seem likely that the beadwork snakes were expressly made for that purpose. More probable is that the Turkish tailors were using what was available to them in the less-than-ideal circumstances.

Some beaded snakes were sold or traded to local families by internees working outside Knockaloe Camp. Two such privately-owned examples were

Photo 21. Detail of three Turkish prisoner-of-war snakes showing variations of the diamond beading pattern.

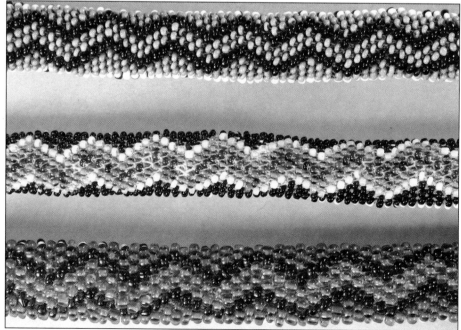

Photo 22. Detail of three Turkish prisoner-of-war snakes showing variations of the zig-zag beading pattern.

included in the Living With the Wire exhibit held at the Manx Museum on the Isle of Man in 1994. The snakes, each measuring over six feet long, were traded to a Manx soldier for bread by Turkish internees working on a land reclamation in 1917. Yvonne Cresswell, the exhibit curator, explained that "The beadwork snakes found on the Isle of Man (of which there are relatively quite a few) are always associated with Knockaloe and not with returning British soldiers. It is interesting to note that very little traditional 'Trench Art' and examples of First World War souvenirs are found on the Island, the vast majority of material being internee craftwork."[16]

SELLING THE CRAFT ITEMS

James Baily and the Society of Friends also undertook the seemingly impossible task of selling the craft items made by the thousands of war prisoners and civilian internees who had to be kept occupied. At first, many of the articles offered to the Friends were beginners' attempts of poor design and craftsmanship that were simply unsuitable for sale. That difficulty was solved by a system of double inspection before a crafted item left the camp–first by the inmate's own industrial committee and then by a Friends' visitor. By the middle of 1915 the Emergency Committee was furthering a standard of quality by "obtaining artistic designs and models from which the men may work."[17]

Photo 23. Three Turkish prisoner-of-war snakes showing different patterns on the heads.

Photo 24. The underside of the same three Turkish prisoner-of-war snake heads.

Ordinary trade markets were closed to selling prisoners' work by a government mandate stating that none of the handicrafts produced in the camps be publicly advertised for sale or placed with any shop or business, so sales had to be personally arranged. To accomplish this task, the Friends kept a good stock of items in a showroom in their London offices "where visitors of all sorts were induced to come and buy"[18] and the general Camp Visitor traveled with cases of articles which he sold at Society of Friends meetings.

The Emergency Committee also arranged for many craft items to be sold outside of Great Britain. A 1917 committee report noted that "large consignments have been shipped to America, where we have received the invaluable and hearty co-operation of the Prisoners of War Relief Committee of New York."[19] Although the Society of Friends hoped to increase the amount of camp-made crafts sent to the United States, shipments ended when America entered the war. The Prisoners of War Relief Committee eventually managed to sell the large quantity of goods sent from England.

The United States was not the only foreign nation to help dispose of prisoners' craft items. In the early part of 1917, the Crown Princess of Sweden organized an exhibit and sale of articles made in the prison camps of England, Germany, and Russia in Stockholm. The Society of Friends sent thirty-three cases of goods from Great Britain, valued at over one thousand pounds, which sold so well that a second exhibition was held at Gothenburg later the same year. Additionally, small craft consignments were sent to Norway and Denmark.

Before the camps in Great Britain closed, the Emergency Committee had sold over twenty thousand pounds worth of the prisoners' handicraft work. While this might not sound like much money today, keep in mind that the items were mostly small things that

Photo 25. Turkish prisoner-of-war snake with a zig-zag pattern made of size 12° beads, dated 1919, measures 55" (140 cm).

sold from a penny upwards and that ordinary trade markets were closed to the prisoners' goods.

Not all of the items produced in the detention camps were given up to the Society of Friends for sale. Men sold, bartered, or gave their work to fellow prisoners and camp officers, made gifts for their wives and children, improved their surroundings in the camps, and made boxes to carry home their belongings.

IN EGYPT

As in Great Britain, beadwork snakes and other souvenirs were also made by Turkish soldiers held in British prison camps in Egypt, India, Salonika, and Mesopotamia but there is little information available on their manufacture. Despite the lack of documentation, it is likely that most of the bead crochet snakes that were made during World War I came from the prison camps in Egypt and neighboring countries. If nothing else, the sheer number of Turkish prisoners in those regions compared with the number of incarcerated men in Great Britain increased the odds of a beadwork snake being made in Egypt. According to eyewitness Bedros M. Sharian, Prisoner of War 31,163, who later served as a translator in the British Army, Heliopolis Camp in Egypt held some 30,000-35,000 prisoners at one point and Bilbeis Camp, also in Egypt, housed some 35,000-40,000 prisoners towards the end of the war. In addition, the stories of

British and Australian soldiers serving in World War I who brought home bead crochet snakes as souvenirs support the idea that most of the prisoner snakes were made in the Middle East.

One direct reference to beadwork production comes from a report on Turkish prisoners in Egypt filed by delegates of the International Red Cross. The delegation visited eight prison camps and two prison hospitals to check on the population, living arrangements, food, exercise, clothing, hygiene, medical attention, work, religion and recreation, correspondence, and prisoners' aid.

While discussing Maadi Camp, the chief camp located about nine miles south of Cairo that held 5,556 prisoners in 1917, the report notes that "some have shown great skill in the manufacture of mandolines, guitars, and tambourines. All materials as well as games are provided gratis by the British Government. Many prisoners make articles of coloured beads–handbags, purses, necklace, bracelets, etc–which show considerable artistic taste. We bought one of these beautiful pieces of work as a specimen. The articles sell readily in the curiosity shops at Cairo. One section of 1,200 prisoners netted from the sales a sum of 2,500 francs in a fortnight."[20]

Although it doesn't mention beadwork specifically, the section of the same report on Bilbeis Camp, situated about forty miles northeast of Cairo and holding about 540 prisoners in 1917, states that "With the exception of fatigue duties, nothing is required from the prisoners besides a little light work in the gardens near the camp. Some of them make small articles which are sold for their benefit."[21]

One such sale was described in an undated newspaper article that accompanied a beaded snake put up for auction. Titled "The Turkish Serpent," the article told the following story:

> The brilliantly-marked snake seen in the accompanying photograph is not quite what it appears to be. Concerning it a nautical reader writes "The snake measures almost five feet in length, and is curled up as though in readiness to strike, but

is actually quite harmless being *made entirely of coloured beads*—about fifty thousand of them—cunningly strung together! This exquisite piece of work was done by a Turkish prisoner-of-war during his spell of captivity in Egypt (1916-1919). Apart from being a draftsman, he must have possessed amazing patience and industry, for this spare-time-job kept him occupied for over two years!"

> Some time after the Armistice, in 1918, I happened to be serving on board the vessel which took him, along with hundreds of others, from Alexandria to Constantinople for repatriation. During the voyage I spent an hour each day with him, bargaining for the serpent, which I greatly

Photo 26. Writing on the underside of two snakes. Note the misspelling of PRISONERS on the bottom snake.

admired. Prices 'hardened', as they say on the Stock Exchange, while the ship was passing through the Dardanelles but shortly before coming to anchor near the Golden Horn we reached an agreement and the bead snake became my property in return for the sum of ten shillings and a few packets of "Woodbines."[22]

Further evidence of beadwork snakes being made by Turkish prisoners can be found in the personal stories of men who served in the Middle-Eastern campaign. Lesleyanne Hawthorne, originally of Melbourne, Australia, recalled that "one of my favorite toys of my childhood was a three-metre intricately beaded snake, made by a Turkish prisoner-of-war for that soldier [her grandfather's brother]. The craftsman wove into it "TURKISH PRISONER 67L," and then the name of my great uncle. Originally, before it got broken, there was a little lizard trapped in the mouth of the snake."[23]

A beadwork snake dated 1915 was brought back to England after the war by Yorkshireman Maurice Kettlewell, who was a cook in a prisoner-of-war camp in Salonika for part of his service in the British Army. Kettlewell was given the snake by one of the prisoners at Salonika in appreciation for his efforts to make sure that the prisoners were well-fed. His daughter remembered that the snake held an honored place in the drawing room and that she and her sisters were occasionally allowed to play with it under very close supervision.[24]

Bits of information about the origins of particular beadwork snakes can be gathered when the snakes are put up

Photo 27. The belly decoration on two Turkish POW snakes.

for sale by family members. One green, pink, white, and black beadwork snake with the phrase "TURKISH PRISON-ERS 1919," offered for sale in 2004, was brought back from Turkey in 1921 by the seller's great-uncle for the seller's great-grandmother, whose totem was the snake. Similar purchases of snake souvenirs might also explain why a number of beaded snakes from the former Ottoman Empire ended up in Native American beadwork collections and were mislabeled as American made.

Another snake put up for auction in 2006 was brought back to the United Kingdom by the seller's great-uncle who was stationed in Egypt during World War I. He bought it as a souvenir some-

Photo 28. Detail of the blue and green snake in Photo 25 showing the thread crochet mouth and separately beaded tongue.

time before 1918 but the family does not remember where in Egypt the soldier was stationed. A third snake with the tantalizing legend "TURKISH PRIS-ONERS CYPRUS 1916" was given to the seller's grandfather, a Canadian soldier who served in the war.

Turkish beaded snakes with dates on them later than the end of the war in1918 are not unusual because the repatriation of Turkish prisoners in Egypt may not have even begun until 1919 and certainly continued until 1921.

The beadwork snakes made in both the Middle-Eastern and English detention camps are so similar in style that there is currently no way to tell where a snake was made by its design. The common characteristics do, however, make it possible to tell a prisoner-of-war snake from one made by other groups.

SNAKE CHARACTERISTICS

Whether the snakes were made in England or Egypt, examination of forty examples shows that there are similarities in construction and design. The reptiles were crocheted from the tail to the tip of the mouth and range in length from thirteen inches (33 cm) on up to eighteen feet (5.5 m) with a common size being around sixty inches (152 cm) long and two to three inches (5–7.5 cm) around.

The particular crochet stitch used to make the snakes was a single crochet rather than a slip stitch. The snakes measuring thirteen inches could have been made by stringing all of the beads at once but longer snakes had to be strung and crocheted in sections, fastening the thread off and on as the work progressed.

Because any bead crochet tube over nine beads around tends to collapse, the larger snakes were stuffed to keep their round shape. Extracting a small amount of stuffing from four snakes in my collection showed a stuffing of fabric in two cases and thin, cotton yarn in two others but stuffing of thread, string, and horsehair have also been reported. The use of yarn as a stuffing material makes sense in light of the machine-knit socks produced at Knockaloe Camp out of unraveled yarn from old socks or new wool. Any unraveled yarn not suitable for knitting new socks could be used for stuffing.

As observers noted at the time, the beadwork snakes were realistically shaped in their proportions; the body gradually grows wider from the tail and then narrows slightly right before the head. The amount decreased before the beginning of the head may be as small as one bead or as large as one-third of the largest amount of beads on the belly. Once the decorative pattern begins on the snake's back, width is added by increasing only the number of beads used for the belly, which is a different color than the top pattern.

These decorative patterns on the top of the snakes are usually either a zig-zag or diamond shape with many variations within either pattern. The zig-zag pattern is, at its simplest, two parallel lines of beads that contrast with the background, such as the black lines on a mauve background seen in Photo 15. Variations might consist of a green background with a zig-zag pattern composed of two black lines separated by a middle line of gold beads as in Photo 19 or a yellow-green background with a zig-zag section made of one line each of blue-green, red, white, red, and blue-green beads.

The diamond pattern consists of a line of diamonds that run up the center of the snake. The diamonds may be connected so that they march one after another or each diamond may be separated by a few rows of the background, as are the diamond patterns in Photo 20. Depending on the diameter of the snake, the diamond motif may be nothing more than a blue diamond with one white bead at the center as in Photo 16 or it may be made up of increasingly smaller lines of bead color, for example blue, white, and a center of gold as in Photo 20. Occasionally, a snake will be found with an all-over diamond pattern on its back.

While a description of the beadwork patterns may give the impression of simplicity, the design of the whole snake can show a surprising level of complexity. The last beads of the zig-zag or diamond pattern on the body might then form two lines that widen on the top of the head until each line ends in a small diamond shape that forms the eyes. A second set of lines decreasing in width might then complete a diamond shape by traveling from the eyes to the tip of the mouth. Alternately, the head may have eyes shaped like flowers and any variety of diamond shapes on the lower part of the head. On the underside of the mouth might be found a diamond, a triangle, a diamond shape within a larger triangle, or a capital A that might signify Allah, all worked in at least one color of contrasting beads. Examples of head designs can be seen in Photos 23 and 24.

The mouths of these beasts are open with bead crochet on the outside and plain thread crochet on the inside with a separate line of contrasting beads dividing the beaded and plain portions, as can be seen in Photo 28. The open mouth is achieved by crocheting each section around separately to make two triangles. Some of the snakes have beaded tongues that are made independently and then fastened to the inside of the mouth; occasionally a snake will be found holding a bead crochet lizard in its mouth, as shown in Photo 29.

Underneath, the snake's belly is usu-

Photo 29. Detail of a Turkish prisoner-of-war snake with a lizard in its mouth. The lizard measures 3″ (7.5 cm) long.

ally made of white beads with black beads used for lettering, although some color other than black may also be used for the writing. Occasionally, colored beads such as yellow or blue are used for the belly in place of the white beads. The upper-case writing on the belly may be as simple as a date like 1919 or may say TURKISH POWS, TP, or TURKISH PRISONER. The main phrase may also be accompanied by a date, a place name (like CYPRUS) or decorations like diamonds or a Union Jack flag. A few snakes have been found with Arabic writing on the belly or the name of the recipient, as with the previously mentioned snake made for Lesleyanne Hawthorne's great uncle. One snake recently offered for sale had the French phrase "PRISONER DE GUERRE 1916" on the belly. That snake was brought back from France by a British soldier serving there during World War I.

Sometimes there are mistakes in the spelling and the legend might read something like "TURKISH PHISONERS 1918." Additionally, occasional backwards letters in the writing or, in one case, an entire phrase with backwards letters can be found. Given that the English phrases were a foreign language to most prisoners and that the beads for the snakes were strung backwards, it is surprising how few mistakes are found. While most of the lettering is found on the belly of a snake, there are examples, like the snake in Photo 14, where a phrase like SOUVENIR was also worked into the pattern on the top of the snake's body.

The common bead colors used to make the decorations are green, topaz, white, black, navy or royal blue, red, mauve, turquoise, and yellow. Thread color is often a neutral tan but can also be a darker brown or dark blue. Occasionally, a snake may start with one color thread and end with another, as if the maker ran out of thread partway through the process.

Regardless of the number of bead colors available, the number of colors in a particular snake is usually restricted to somewhere between three and seven with four or five colors per snake being most common. A three-color snake pattern might consist of black lines that zig-zag through a mauve background on top with a white belly that frames black lettering underneath. A five-color pattern might consist of a white belly, blue diamonds with white centers on a green background for the top pattern, red centers in white eyes and yellow centers in blue diamonds on the head. The size of the snake does not correspond to the number of bead colors used. The five-color pattern described above is found on a snake measuring twenty-one inches (53 cm) while the three-color pattern mentioned above is found on a snake measuring sixty-six inches (167 cm).

As with bead color, the size of the seed beads used for the snakes varies.

Photo 30. Two World War I, Turkish prisoner-of-war lizards showing different diamond patterns. *Left,* measures 7½″ (19 cm), *right,* measures 9½″ (24 cm).

The exact bead size can be a bit difficult to pin down because the individual beads produced were not as uniform in size as they are today and prisoners apparently used every bead available, even those that were clearly smaller than the norm. That said, the largest bead used for some of the snakes corresponds to a modern size 6° seed bead; the most common size was one that most closely corresponds to a modern size 8° seed bead. Occasionally two sizes of beads would be combined in one snake to make part of the design stand out. One such snake, seen on the left in Photo 23, has size 8° beads for the two prominent white lines that zig-zag through a background of size 9° or 10° dark blue beads. Some snakes were even made with size 12° beads, although the smaller beads were not necessarily used to make shorter snakes. A thirteen-inch snake (33 cm) could use size 9° beads while one measuring fifty-five inches (140 cm) can be made with size 12° beads, like the snake in Photo 25. Thread size corresponds to bead size so a smaller crochet thread was used with size 12° beads than with size 6° beads.

LIZARD CHARACTERISTICS

Rarer than any style of beadwork snake are the bead crochet lizards made by the Turkish prisoners of war;

my research counted four World War I snakes for every lizard from the same period. Found clutched in a snake's mouth or standing on their own, the lizards show the same characteristics as the beadwork snakes.

The bodies, legs, and sometimes even the claws are made with the same single crochet method used for the snakes. The heads with open mouths are also constructed so that the outside of the head has beads on it while the inside is plain thread crochet. Inside and outside of the mouth are divided by a row of beads in contrasting color and some of the lizards have beaded tongues. The underside of the head may also have a triangle design worked in two or three bead colors.

Like the snakes, the lizards vary both in their overall length and the size of beads used in their construction.

The overall length ranges from three and one-half inches to nine inches (9 cm-23 cm) with a common size being a little over seven inches (18 cm). Bead size ranges from 12° to 9°. Some lizards are found with dates worked in beads on the underside of the body.

Patterns used for the body include a single diamond, a series of diamonds as seen on the two lizards of Photo 30,

Photo 31. Detail of the lizards' mouths. *Left,* the mouth is thread crochet that has been painted red. *Right,* the mouth is thread crochet with a beaded tongue attached.

Photo 32. Underside of the two lizards shown in Photo 30. *Top,* the green lizard employs a mixture of bead colors to produce the variegated effect on the belly. *Bottom,* the date 1916 is worked in beads.

zig-zag lines as on the lizard in Photo 29, or dotted lines. The heads may have a flower motif or diamonds for eyes. Some lizards, like the one on the left in Photo 30, combine both diamond and flower motifs on the head with flowers for the eyes and a small diamond motif further down towards the point of the mouth. While the number of bead colors used in the patterns ranged from four to nine, the common number of colors used was about five.

Both the larger and smaller lizards, even those caught in the mouths of snakes, have a thick wire that runs from neck to tail that serves to keep the head and tail from drooping. Since the lizards were meant to stand on their little bead-crocheted legs, the limbs also have wire supports in them. A thinner wire, similar to a modern 28- or 30-gauge craft wire, was used to stiffen bead crocheted claws or to make loops of strung beads that simulate claws.

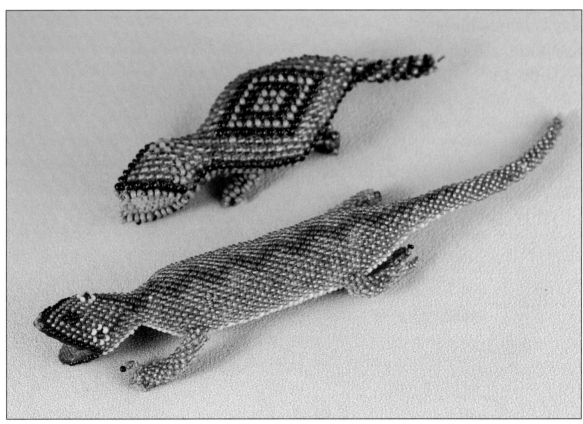

Photo 33. Two bead crochet lizards made by Turkish prisoners of war during World War I. *Top,* measures 5″ (12.5 cm), *bottom,* measures 7½″ (19 cm). Photo by Jane Kimball.

Photo 34. Old civilian-made snake with a pattern that incorporates a zig-zag line moving between a flower motif, measuring 26″ (66 cm) from tip to nose. Note the security loop attached at the mouth to help the leader of a line dance keep a grip on the snake.

CIVILIAN-MADE SNAKES

After the First World War, women in rural parts of Southeastern Europe began to make bead crochet snakes for family use. This group of snakes has no connection with World War I internment camps, but is rather associated by oral tradition with parts of Macedonia and Greece. Most of these bead crochet snakes were made during the period between the two World Wars but some snakes were produced up through the 1970s.

These bead crochet snakes were made in villages to be used as part of a line dance or given as an engagement present from a girl to her fiancé. Snakes sold as souvenirs in town markets tend to be less intricate in design and thinner than the ones made for local use. These civilian-made beaded serpents are often mistakenly sold as a World War I prisoner-of-war item but examination of twenty-four snakes shows that they are stylistically a group unto themselves.

Like the prisoner-of-war snakes, the village-made snakes were done with a bead single crochet stitch and stuffed to stiffen the piece. The rural artisans, however, had access to a form of loose cotton similar to cosmetic cotton balls and used that in place of old fabric and yarn bits to stuff their beadwork snakes.

Civilian-made snakes range in length from eighteen and one-half inches to twenty-nine inches (47 cm-73.5 cm) and measure from three-quarters of an inch to two and three-quarters of an inch (2 cm–7 cm) around at the widest part of the body. The snakes are made with size 10° or 12° seed beads. While some of the village-made snakes mimic real snakes in shape by increasing the width of the body gradually from the tail and decreasing width slightly before the head, most show a more fanciful shape. On these snakes, the tail remains slender for about one-quarter of the length of the body and then widens rather rapidly to its full circumference and does not decrease in width towards the head. One such example can be seen in Photo 34. As a further decorative element, the end of the tail may sport a series of loops or an oval bobble.

The most common beadwork patterns on the top side of the snakes con-

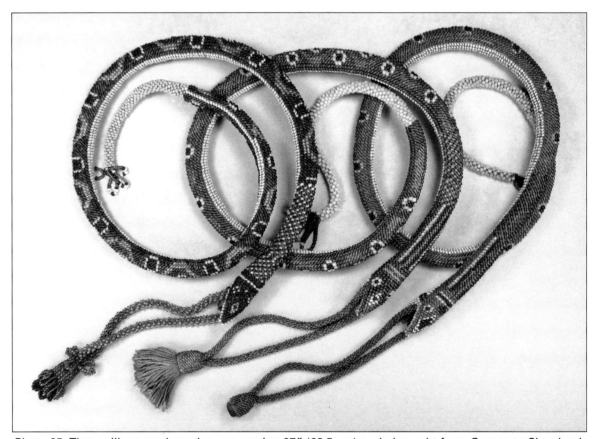

Photo 35. Three village-made snakes, measuring 27″ (68.5 cm) each, brought from Greece to Cleveland, Ohio sometime between 1917 and 1943 by an American woman married to a Greek man. The snake on the right uses the same zig-zag line between flowers pattern as the other two snakes, but the bead color for the zig-zag line is too close to the background color for the pattern to be visible.

sist of either flowers set among a central zig-zag line like the examples seen in Photo 36 or a line of oval medallions that run up the center of the body, as in Photo 37. The upper portion of the body before the head would have vertical stripes, a checkerboard pattern, horizontal stripes, or any combination thereof. Patterns are composed of more bead colors than the prisoner-of-war snakes and use from five to nine separate colors. Thread colors on examined snakes range from medium brown or tan on the older snakes to white on the newer snakes. Older snakes are made with cotton crochet thread while newer ones may be done with nylon thread.

Like the prisoner-of-war snakes, the village-made snakes have a separately colored belly section but the width is smaller and no writing is incorporated into belly design. While yellow is a common color, the snakes may also sport bellies with colors such as white, green, clear opalescent, or blue.

The head of the snake may have an open or closed mouth. Like its wartime counterpart, a snake with an open mouth will have beads on the outside of the head and plain crochet on the inside of the mouth with a row of contrasting beads separating the two parts. The mouth can also have a beaded tongue. The village-made snake may have a bead crochet handle attached to the edges of the mouth that allows the user to securely hold on to the snake while twirling it as he leads a dance line.

Photo 36. Detail of three variations of the pattern employing a zig-zag line among flower motifs.

Photo 37. Old, civilian-made snake with a medallion pattern, measuring 21" (53.5 cm). This snake does not appear to have ever had a security loop at the mouth.

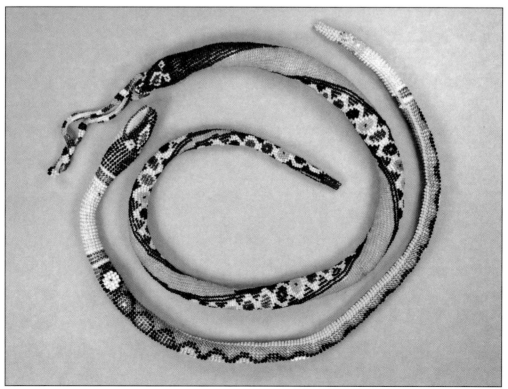

Photo 38. Two civilian-made snakes that were made more recently than the previously pictured snakes. Both use the medallion pattern.
Top, over-stuffed snake measuring 30" (76 cm) with a security loop.
Bottom, a snake measuring 27" (68.5 cm) with no security loop.

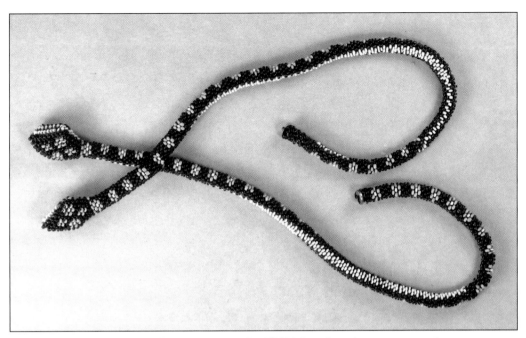

Photo 39. Two flower-patterned, 12" (30.5 cm) snakes sewn together to make a necklace that fastens with a dressmaker's snap. Each snake has a two-part mouth and beaded tongue like its larger counterparts.

SOUVENIR SNAKES AND JEWELRY

The same women who made snakes for their own villages were part of a larger group who produced bead crochet snakes in the form of souvenirs or jewelry. The snakes in this category were made by a number of people including rural women selling snakes at town markets, women making snake necklaces as a part of a cottage industry, homemakers beading snakes as "fancy work," and civilian prisoners in Turkish jails.

By the 1920s there was enough general interest in beadwork snakes that at least one ladies' needlework magazine published a pattern for a bead crochet snake bracelet. *Leach's Beadwork, Beautiful Designs for Bags, Hats, and Frock trimmings, Necklaces, Girdles, and Other Useful Articles* contains instructions for what is described as a "Realistic Snake Girdle or Armband"[25] but is, in reality, a small version of the beadwork snakes found in the Balkans. The pattern instructs the reader to crochet the snake in a tube until the divide for the jaws on the head, at which point each half of the head is crocheted flat. The reader is directed to fasten on the thread, crochet across the row, cut the thread, fasten off the thread and repeat the sequence for each row. After all of the rows were finished, the pattern instructs the reader to tie the threads securely and line the mouth with silk.

Strangely enough, the illustration for the "Realistic Snake Girdle" shows the snake wound around the arm from wrist to just below the elbow but following the pattern gives you a snake that is meant to go once around the wrist. The pattern further deviates from the illustration with instructions to sew a snap on the inside of the mouth so that the bracelet can be fastened on the wrist by placing the tail in the mouth and closing the snap. There are no instructions for making a snake to match the drawing. Photo 40 shows the illustration accompanying the pattern and the snake resulting from following the instructions.

Aside from those produced by following Mrs. Leach's bracelet pattern, most of the snakes meant to be worn as

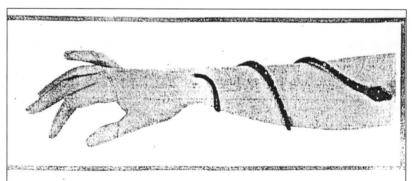

Photo 40. Illustration from the bead crochet snake pattern shown in *Leach's Beadwork* and the snake that results from following the pattern. Although the snake in the illustration winds up the arm, the actual snake is only long enough to go around the wrist.

jewelry range in length from nineteen to twenty-six inches (48 cm-66 cm), long enough to be worn as a necklace. The beads used are size 10° to 12° and the snakes are only about nine or ten beads around at the widest point of the body. The common beadwork pattern, seen on the snakes in Photo 41, is a flower motif separated by plain rows with one horizontal row of contrasting beads separating the flower pattern and the beginning of the head.

The head of such snakes has an open mouth with beads on the outside and plain thread crochet on the inside of the mouth like the larger versions and may or may not have a contrasting row of beads separating inside and out. Neither the mouth nor the body contain any stuffing. This type of snake does not necessarily have a belly with beads of a different color from the top. The number of bead colors is small, ranging from two to four colors per snake, but more thread colors are used so that the thread more closely matches the beads. The tails may be plain, have beaded loops, or end in twisted fringe.

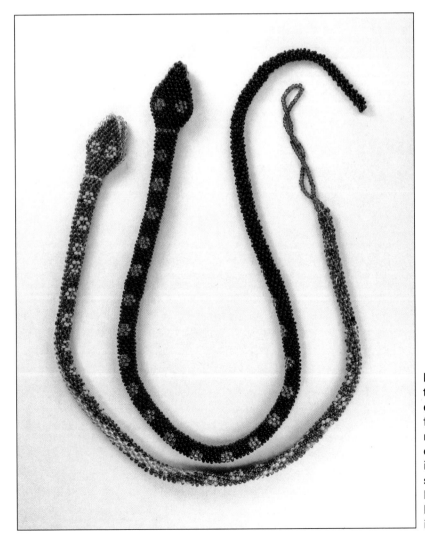

Photo 41. Two snakes made to be worn as necklaces employing the common flower pattern. *Top,* this snake, measuring a little over 19" (48 cm), retains its metal fastener in the mouth. *Bottom,* this snake, measuring 19" (48 cm), has lost its metal fastener but retains the thread where it was sewn to the snake.

Photo 39 shows an imaginative use of the flower-motif snake by sewing together two twelve-inch snakes to make one necklace that fastens at the tails with a dressmaker's snap. Along with the flower motif on the back, these twin snakes sport white bellies, diamond motifs on the heads, tongues, and triangle motifs on the underside of the mouth. The use of a dressmaker's snap to fasten the necklace indicates that the necklace was not commercially made.

Photo 42. Detail of the mouths of the snake necklaces in Photo 41. *Top,* the spring-operated metal fastener that would grab on to the tail to make a loop for a necklace. *Bottom,* plain crochet mouth from the snake that has lost its fastener.

Some of the snakes are clearly meant to be worn as necklaces because their mouths contain a sophisticated metal closure that is sewn in after the snake is finished. Photo 42 shows such a spring-loaded closure with sharp, metal teeth top and bottom so that the mouth can clamp around the tail and stay in place. The head on these snakes is wider than other examples because it has to conform to the size of the metal closure.

937. BALKAN TYPEN - Unsere Feldgrauen auf dem Spitzenmarkt in Mazedonien.

Photo 43. Postcard showing German soldiers shopping at a village market in Macedonia. Original photo taken by O. Miehlmann, Hamburg.

Photo 44.
Snake rosary
made by a
civilian prisoner
in Turkey,
tentatively
dated as 1970s.
The piece
measures
15" (38 cm),
including the
decoration
at the tail.

Photo 45. Snake that was made and sold as a souvenir in Algeria
and brought back to England in the 1970s, measures 33" (84 cm).

This type of snake jewelry was still being sold as late as the 1960s.

A few vintage bead crochet snakes made by Turkish civilian prisoners have recently shown up on the market. As can be seen from the thirty-year-old example in Photo 44, this type of simplified snake has more in common with the later snakes made for jewelry than with the Turkish prisoner-of-war snakes. In this example, the mouth is crocheted in one piece so that it does not open but it does sport a fanciful triangle at the end.

Examples of more complicated snake souvenirs can occasionally surface. Photo 45 shows a snake that was bought in Algeria by an Englishman traveling on business in the 1970s; while the beading pattern is simple, the snake exhibits a lot of personality. A more curious souvenir in the form of a riding crop with a snake's head at the tip can be seen in Photo 46.

Photo 46. Bead crochet riding crop with a snake's head on the end, date unknown, measuring 20″ (51 cm) excluding the beaded security loop. The snake's mouth is done in two parts and has thread crochet on the inside like the larger snakes.

Photo 47. Bead crochet snake measuring 33″
(84 cm) made by Yoshie Marubashi.

SNAKES TODAY

With the increased industrialization of Europe and lure of all things modern, the tradition of bead crochet snakes slowly fell out of favor in the 1950s and 1960s. In England, Australia, and the United States, what had been treasured keepsakes of service in World War I or travel in the Balkan countries became strange knick-knacks stuck in attics by descendants who had no interest in such folk art. As the original owners died off, the stories behind such beaded items were lost.

Today these same beadwork snakes and lizards are coming up for sale as antiques but the lack of documentation is causing much confusion about their origins. Simply because of the small seed beads used, the snakes are often mistakenly labeled as Victorian or Native American. There is no evidence to date that Victorian ladies made bead crochet snakes and, although some American Indians were taught needlework and crochet as part of assimilation attempts by the United States government, I have yet to find a Native American tribe that counts bead crochet as a traditional technique. At the same time, sellers are labeling any beadwork snake as made by Turkish prisoners of war during World War I.

In reality, bead crochet snakes may have a common construction method but come in a variety of styles and were made in various countries at different times. If you are purchasing a beadwork snake, you may have to play detective to determine the story behind the coveted reptile. What kind of thread was used to crochet the beads? Nylon thread is shinier than cotton and indicates a newer snake. What size beads were used? Turkish prisoners often used larger beads and fewer colors but Balkan villagers and jewelry makers used smaller beads and more colors. Souvenir snakes often show simpler patterns than those made for personal use. Was the snake kept with other items that can give a clue as to date? If the snake was stored with some World War I medals, that would give an indication as to age. Sometimes questions about the original owner's nationality or travels will give the buyer informa-

tion about the snake in question.

What began as way for prisoners to pass time under trying conditions, insure a happy marriage, or make a little money is now being valued as a form of folk art. The beaded snakes and lizards have become highly collectible, appealing to both beadwork and military collectors. Additionally the craft of bead crochet has recently regained popularity among American, British, Japanese, and German beaders as well as crochet enthusiasts who are anxious to add beads to their fiber work. Although instructions for tubular bracelets and necklaces abound, there are currently only a few bead artists in the United States and Germany exploring bead crochet snakes. The enthusiastic response to my snake jewelry indicates that there are many more people who would like to make their own shiny serpent. If you are one of those souls, turn the page and get started.

Photo 48. Three bead crochet snakes made by Miriam Milgram as part of a series of forty-nine snakes. The snakes range in size from 18 1/2″ (47 cm) to 21″ (53.5 cm).

NOTES

1. Fanny Janet Blunt and Stanley Lane-Poole (editor), *The people of Turkey: twenty years residence among Bulgarians, Greek, Albanians, Turks, and Armenians* (London: John Murray, 1878), 98 and 112.

2. Maude Rea Parkinson, *Twenty Years in Roumania* (London: G. Allen & Unwin, 1921), 232.

3. Burton Holmes, *Burton Holmes travelogues: with illustrations from photographs by the author* (New York: The McClure Co., 1910), 52.

4. Miriam Milgram, *Balkan Beaded Crochet* (New York: Miriam Milgram, 1998), 4.

5. Anita Csukovits, "Art under pressure–Artifacts of Hungarian prisoners in the 19-20th century showed in the exhibition room of the Greek Tempel in Vac," *Neprajzi ertesito. Annales Musei ethnographiae* 84 (2002): 145.

6. Holly Edwards, "Ex-Iraqi prisoner threaded beauty in midst of suffering," *Tennessean*, May 12, 2003, *http://www.tennessean.com*

7. Sadik Saigiroglu, email message to author, February 4, 2006.

8. Robert Means Lawrence, *The magic of the horse-shoe, with other folk-lore notes,* (Detroit, Michigan: Singing Tree Press, 1968), 63.

9. George Oprescu, *Peasant Art in Roumania,* (London: The Studio, 1929), 16.

10. Republic of Turkey Ministry of Culture and Tourism, "Beliefs: Good Luck-Bad Luck," *http://www.kultur.gov.tr*

11. Olive Lodge, "Folk Festivals in Yugoslavia," *Folklore,* 55, No. 2 (June, 1944): 62.

12. M.E. Durham, *Some tribal origins, laws, and customs of the Balkans* (London: George Allen & Unwin Ltd., 1928), 245.

13. OliveLodge, "Folk Festivals in Yugoslavia," *Folklore,* 55, No. 2 (June, 1944): 62.

14. "British Treatment of enemy Prisoners," *Manx Quarterly #17,* (October, 1916), *http://www.isle-of-man.com/manxnotebook/mquart/mq17071.htm.*

15. Frank C. Quayle, "Knockaloe Moar," *Isle of Man Family History Society Journal,* 12, No. 4 (1990) *http://www.isle-of-man.com/manxnotebook/famhist/v12n4.htm.#128-130*

16 Yvonne Cresswell, email message to author, March 18, 2005.

17. Emergency Committee for the Assistance of Germans, Austrians, and Hungarians in Distress, *Report,* (June 30, 1915): 10.

18. Anna Braithwaite Thomas, *St. Stephen's House: Friends' Emergency Work in England 1914–1920* (London: Emergency Committee for the Assistance of Germans, Austrians, and Hungarians in Distress, ca. 1920), 70.

19. Emergency Committee for the Assistance of Germans, Austrians, and Hungarians in Distress, *Report,* (June 30, 1917): 7.

20. International Committee of the Red Cross, *Turkish Prisoners in Egypt* (London: Cassell & Co., 1917), 24-25.

21. Ibid., 58.

22. Jane Kimball, *Trench Art: An Illustrated History* (Davis, California: Silverpenny Press, 2004), 269.

23. Lesleyanne Hawthorne, *Johnny Turk* (Melbourne, Australia: ATFS Publications, 1986), *http://www.atmg.org*

24. Kimball, *Trench Art: An Illustrated History,* 246.

25. Stephany Tomalin, "Crocheted Snakes," *Bead Society of Great Britain Newsletter,* 30 (September, 1995): 20.

Projects

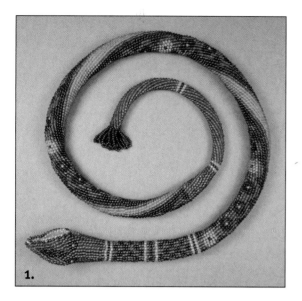

1.

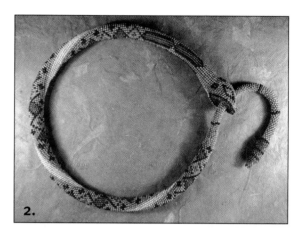

2.

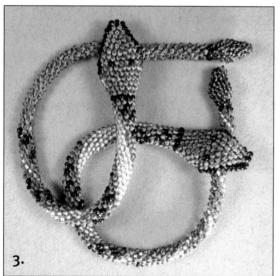

3.

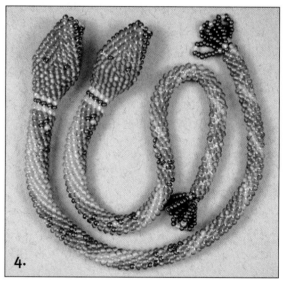

4.

5.

1: Green Snake Necklace, p. 67

2: Rattlesnake Necklace, p. 77

3: Rattlesnake Bracelet, p. 85

4: Green Snake Bracelet, p. 92

5: Memory Wire Snake Bracelet, p. 99

GETTING STARTED

IN GENERAL

These patterns are written for someone who has already made a few tubular bead crochet bracelets or necklaces using a slip stitch or single crochet stitch. The snakes are crocheted from tail to head using bead single crochet–a stitch that is clearly outlined in the book. In addition you will learn an alternate stringing method, how to increase and decrease a bead, and how to crochet on both sides of a foundation chain.

CHOOSING BEADS

I love to combine any seed beads that appeal to me, so the snakes use a mixture of Matsuno and Czech seed beads. Bead uniformity is not as much of a concern with bead crochet as it is with other beadwork techniques, so you can often use a combination of size 10°, size 11°, and/or size 12° beads without a problem.

Listing the bead colors used for the snake patterns has been a challenge because there seems to be little standardization of color numbers or names. For instance, the green Matsuno beads used for the first snake are listed as color 22FAB in two of the Japanese bead stores that I shop at in New York City but are called "Emerald" at a website store that carries Japanese beads. The yellow Czech beads used for the belly of the green snake are referred to as "topaz" at stores that sell beads to garment manufacturers and "yellow" at retail stores. In case it will be of any help to those of you who **57** want to purchase the same beads that I used in the snakes, I have included the Matsuno color numbers used by retail stores in Manhattan as a loose guide.

I also have a habit of buying beads that appeal to me and squirreling them away until the right project comes along, so it may be hard for you to find the exact striped beads that I used for the rattlesnake. This may not be a major problem because, if you are experienced enough to tackle a beaded snake, you probably have your own color scheme in mind.

THREAD

The patterns were designed for size 30 cotton crochet thread, preferably Cebelia by DMC. A lot of people prefer Silamide, Jeans Stitch, or Guterman topstitching thread but be warned that using those threads will result in a thinner and shorter snake. You may have to add motifs to achieve the same final length as the pattern.

STRINGING METHOD

Patterns normally tell you to string beads directly onto the crochet thread going backwards so that the first bead strung is the last bead crocheted but doing that on a large project like a snake necklace leads to a giant headache. Given the changing body size and multiple patterns, as well as the fact that the snake necklaces are too long to be strung in one go anyway, it is easier to string the beads in the order in which they will be used. To accomplish that, you will string the beads needed for a section onto sewing thread in the order listed so that the first bead strung is the first bead crocheted. You will then transfer the beads to the size 30 crochet thread and be ready to start crocheting.

The beads for the small snake bracelet can be strung all at one time but the necklaces and memory wire bracelet need to be strung in sections. Stringing 40"-45" (102 cm-115 cm) of beads on the sewing thread is a comfortable amount to crochet with at one time.

BEAD SINGLE CROCHET

There are a few ways to do bead single crochet and the particular method employed will affect the feel of the snake's body, the alignment of the beads, and the designs possible. If you don't yet know how to do bead single crochet, there are instructions in the Technique Section. Those beaders interested in exploring bead crochet design will find an illustrated discussion of four bead single crochet methods at the end of the Techniques Section.

When you are crocheting a snake, make sure that you only go through the one outside loop of the row underneath; if you go through both loops (as you do with slip stitch) the snake will be too stiff and won't drape nicely.

READING THE PATTERNS

I tried to come up with a pattern system that both right-handed as well as my fellow left-handed beaders could follow. The best compromise was to read the patterns top to bottom, left to right, as you would a book. The stringing starts with the first bead on the left in Row 1 of any pattern.

To make the patterns less confusing, I have divided a snake into sections. The Tail refers to the beginning tube, such as the 9-around on the necklaces. On the necklaces, the Lower Body Increase is the section that increases quickly and the Lower Body is the longest pattern section, either medallions or diamonds. The Upper Body is the pattern section between the lower body and the head, like the checkerboard pattern. The Neck is the section that increases before the divide for the mouth, the Top of the Head has the eyes in it and the Bottom of the Head is the jaw.

A NOTE ON GAUGE

Trying to measure something as small as 9 beads around does not lead to the most accurate gauge but the tail of the two larger snakes should measure about $5/8$" (1.5 cm) around and the lower body should measure about $1^1/8$" (2.8 cm) around. Also, the size of the beads will make a small difference but if your beads lie smoothly and are not bunching up or if there is not a lot of thread showing, your work should be close to the stated gauge. I have given a measurement from Tail to end of the Lower Body so that you can adjust your snake to match the pattern. You can add or subtract motifs to make your snake match the stated length.

STARTING THE TAIL

If you have trouble crocheting the beginning rows of a tail that has no pattern in it, there are two tricks that will help. First, it may be easier to crochet around a support. A toothpick works well for the 5 or 6 around tails of the snake bracelets while a dowel or short knitting needle may work for the 9 around tail of the necklaces. If you are still having trouble figuring out which loop to crochet into next, count the chains backwards from the hook. Do not count the loop on the crochet hook.

TO STUFF THE SNAKE OR NOT

On the two larger snakes, the crocheted tube will flatten out as the body gets wider. If this bothers you, the snake body can be supported by lightly stuffing it as you crochet with small amounts of polyester fiberfill used to make stuffed toys. Each type of construction has its pluses and minuses. A snake with no stuffing drapes nicely around the neck and feels more sinuous in the hand but the tube collapses so that the snake looks flat. A stuffed snake keeps its round

Photo 49. *Top,* green snake necklace without stuffing; *bottom,* green snake necklace with stuffing. Notice that the snake without stuffing bends more but is flatter in shape.

shape but loses some of the drape. Compare the difference between the two snakes with and without stuffing in Photo 49.

Since polyester fiberfill can be a bit unruly, here is one method to make the stuffing process easier. Use your thumb and first finger to pinch off a small amount of fiberfill. Pull the piece of fiberfill at each end so that you have more of a rope shape. Twist the fiberfill (the twists won't stay but it will help tame the fibers). Fold over one end of the "rope" and place it in the opening of the crocheted snake body. Using the smooth end of a crochet hook, push the fiberfill into the snake until it supports the tube. If you stuff the tube too tightly, take the crochet hook and pull the stuffing up a bit.

Be careful not to put too much stuffing in your snake or it will not drape nicely. Also, don't let the stuffing get too close to the row you are crocheting or the fibers will get caught up in your stitches. You can lightly stuff the snake's head if you wish, but it isn't necessary.

RESOURCES FOR CEBELIA THREAD

If your local yarn shop does not carry size 30 Cebelia crochet thread, it can be ordered from the companies below. Herrschners and Mary Maxim have color charts on their websites and in their catalogues that can give you a general idea of the thread color.
- Herrschners: (800) 441-0838 or *www.herrschners.com*
- Handy Hands: (217) 379-3802 or *www.hhtatting.com*
- Lacis: (510) 843-7178 or *www.lacis.com*
- Mary Maxim: (800) 962-9504 or *www.marymaxim.com*

NOTE: You may use any size 30 cotton but Cebelia works best for this type of crocheting with beads. If you need to check exact colors before you order them, the Cebelia color numbers correspond to DMC floss colors so any store that sells embroidery floss should have a color chart.

ALTIN BASAK TURKISH THREAD

This is a Turkish cotton crochet thread that comes in a large number of colors. The size 50 is similar to the American size 30 crochet thread.
- Gentile Lace: (360) 715-3682 or *www.tattingreborn.com*
- Country Closet: (866) 380-8737 or *www.thethreadstore.com.*
- Threads Galore: 01332 383841 or *www.threads-galore.co.uk*

TECHNIQUES

TRANSFERRING BEADS TO CEBELIA THREAD

1. Leaving a 6"(15 cm) tail, make an overhand knot in the sewing thread but don't pull tight.

2. Put the end of the size 30 crochet thread through the open loop, leaving a 6" (15 cm) tail on the crochet thread.

3. Pull the knot in the sewing thread tight. Holding both of the thread tails against the crochet cotton, carefully slide the beads over the knot onto the crochet cotton (Figure 1).

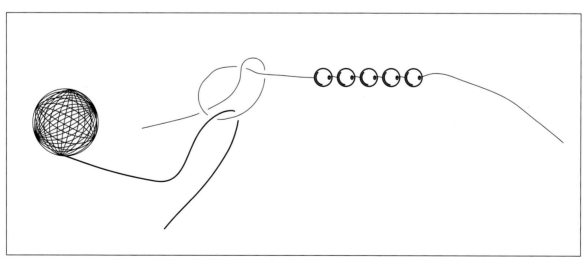

Figure 1. Transferring beads from sewing thread to crochet thread.

RIGHT-HANDED BEAD
SINGLE CROCHET

1. Insert the crochet hook through the top thread loop of the first chain (Figure 2R).

2. Wrap the thread over the hook once (called a yarn over) and draw the thread through the work so that you have 2 loops on the hook.

3. Slide one bead down, push it firmly against the work, and yarn over (Figure 3R). NOTE: The bead in the illustration has not been pushed down all of the way so that it is easier to see.

4. Draw the thread through both of the loops on the hook to finish the stitch (Figure 4R).

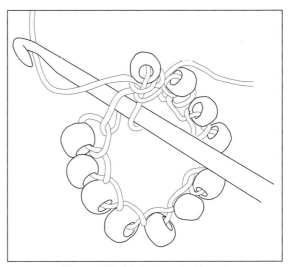

Figure 2R. Right-handed bead single crochet, step 1.

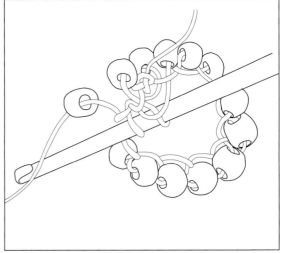

Figure 3R. Right-handed bead single crochet, steps 2–3.

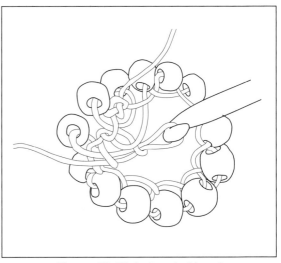

Figure 4R. Right-handed bead single crochet, step 4.

LEFT-HANDED BEAD SINGLE CROCHET

1. Insert the crochet hook through the top thread loop of the first chain (Figure 2L).

2. Wrap the thread over the hook once (called a yarn over) and draw the thread through the work so that you have 2 loops on the hook.

3. Slide one bead down, push it firmly against the work, and yarn over (Figure 3L). NOTE: The bead in the illustration has not been pushed down all of the way so that it is easier to see.

4. Draw the thread through both of the loops on the hook to finish the stitch (Figure 4L).

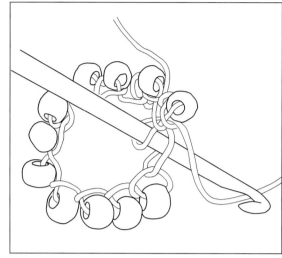

Figure 2L. Left-handed bead single crochet, step 1.

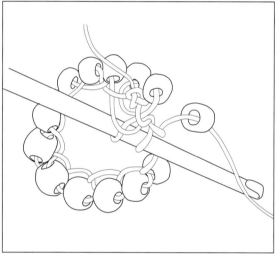

Figure 3L. Left-handed bead single crochet, steps 2–3.

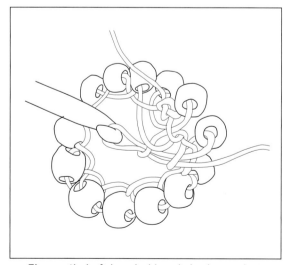

Figure 4L. Left-handed bead single crochet, step 4.

INCREASING THE NUMBER OF BEADS IN A ROW

1. Bead single crochet in one thread loop as usual.
2. Bead single crochet the second bead in the same loop as the first bead (Figure 5).

DECREASING THE NUMBER OF BEADS IN A ROW

1. Bead single crochet in the first loop as usual.
2. Skip the next loop.
3. Bead single crochet in the third loop (Figure 6).

JOINING A NEW THREAD

Here are two methods of joining a new thread to the bead crochet project. Method A is easier overall and can be used on small bead tubes like the snake bracelets. Method B looks nicer but is a little bit more work and can't be used in small bead tubes.

Method A

1. When you run out of beads, cut the crochet thread, leaving a 3" (7.5 cm) tail.
2. Make 1 chain without a bead in it. Pull the tail through and tighten into a knot.
3. Transfer the next section of beads from the sewing thread to the crochet thread.
4. Leaving a 3" tail, make a slip knot on the end of the new crochet thread and place it on the crochet hook.

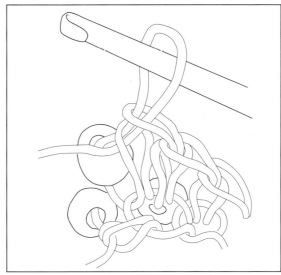

Figure 5. Increasing.

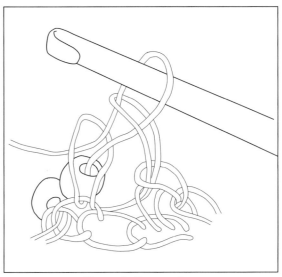

Figure 6. Decreasing.

5. Put the hook through the loop of your last crocheted bead on the snake.
6. Yarn over and pull the thread through the loop and the slip knot. Tighten up the slip knot.
7. Continue crocheting around, stopping at some point to pull the tail left on the outside to the inside of the snake.

Method B

1. When you run out of beads, cut the thread leaving a 3" (7.5 cm) tail. Set the beadwork aside.

2. Transfer the next section of beads from the sewing thread to the crochet cotton.

3. Return to the beadwork and, holding both the old and new thread tails together, start crocheting with the new thread and beads.

4. After you have crocheted the next row and a half, stop and go back to the join.

5. Pull both tails to the inside of the work with your crochet hook and adjust the tension of the stitches.

6. Thread each tail separately onto a needle and make a knot on a chain below the current row.

7. Stuff the tails down inside the tube.

DESIGNING WITH BEAD SINGLE CROCHET

For those who want to design their own patterns, the method used to complete a bead single crochet stitch makes a difference in the final product. It can affect the amount that the pattern spirals around the tube, the length of the tube, the stiffness of the tube, and even the type of pattern that you can use. The variations involve whether you take your hook through one or both thread loops in the chain and whether you pull a bead down before or after the first yarn over.

Photo 50 shows samples of the same pattern worked in four different methods of bead single crochet. Sample A, first on the left of the photo, is done by putting the crochet hook through only one thread loop, sliding a bead down, doing

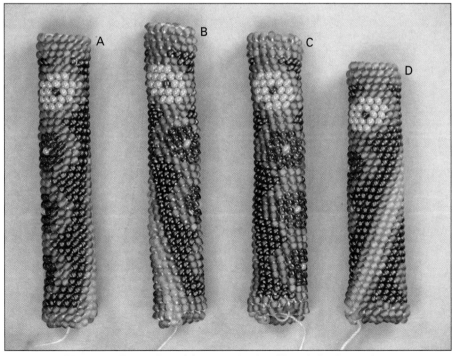

Photo 50. Examples of four methods of bead single crochet.

one yarn over, pulling the yarn over through the thread loop, then pulling a second yarn over through both loops on the hook. The individual beads in a row sit at an angle and show less of the crochet thread. This method produces a tube that drapes nicely and has the least amount of pattern spiraling of any of the four bead single crochet methods. When designing a pattern, regular graph paper can be used.

Sample B, second from the left in the photo, is made by putting the crochet hook through only one thread loop, doing a yarn over, pulling the yarn over through the thread loop, sliding a bead down, then pulling a second yarn over through both loops to complete the stitch. A tube done in this method has a nice drape but will be longer than one done by Method A. The individual beads in each row are not angled like they are in Sample A but instead sit flat with the hole aligned vertically and show more of the crochet thread. The pattern spirals around a medium amount. When designing for this method, regular graph paper can be used.

Sample C, third from the left, is accomplished by putting the crochet hook through both thread loops, sliding a bead down, doing the first yarn over, pulling the yarn over through the thread loop, then pulling the second yarn over through both loops on the hook. The tube feels a bit more substantial than

the first two samples but is shorter than Sample B. Like Sample B, the individual beads sit perpendicular to the top of the work with more thread showing but the pattern spirals less. When designing for this method, regular graph paper can be used.

Sample D, on the right of the photo, is done by putting the crochet hook through both thread loops, sliding a bead down, doing one yarn over, pulling the yarn over through both thread loops, then pulling a second yarn over through both loops on the hook. Like Sample C the resulting tube is more substantial than those done by going through only one thread loop and it is the shortest sample of the group. The individual beads in a row sit at an angle but they also do not line up vertically with the bead below them; rather the beads move over half a bead as they do in bead slip stitch. This results in a distorted pattern that spirals the most. When designing for this method, you must use pattern paper where each row is offset by half a bead such as a graph for bead slip stitch or brick stitch.

I chose to use the bead single crochet method that produced Sample B to make the snakes in this book. That method results in a sinuous body that will drape nicely around your neck or wrist. This method produces a tube that drapes nicely and shows some spiraling of the pattern for added interest.

Green
Snake
Necklace

This is one half of *The Twins* seen in *500 Beaded Objects*. The tail starts with a 9 around tube and increases from there. If you want to wear the snake as a necklace, follow the suggestions at the end of the pattern.

MATERIALS

24 grams size 12° Japanese green seed beads (Matsuno 22FAB)

20 grams size 12° Japanese copper seed beads (Matsuno 176)

5 grams size 12° Japanese purple seed beads (Matsuno 13/207)

3 grams size 12° Japanese salmon seed beads (Matsuno 9F)

1 hank size 10° Czech yellow (topaz) seed beads (or size 12° Matsuno 1)

2 strands (from 1 hank) size 10° or 11° Czech light blue seed beads

1 ball of green DMC Cebelia size 30 cotton crochet thread (color 955)

1 spool sewing thread (any kind) for stringing

Small amount of polyester fiberfill (optional)

TOOLS

1 size 10 (1.30 mm) or 11 (1.10 mm) steel crochet hook

Size 10 beading needles for stringing

Size 7 sharps sewing needles

GAUGE

13–14 beads around = 1" (2.5 cm)

12 rows = 1" (2.5 cm)

Measurement from start of Tail to end of Lower Body (laid flat) = 25¼" (64 cm)

STRINGING THE TAIL BEADS AND LOWER BODY INCREASE

1. String the following onto the sewing thread:

First tail section:

279 green beads, 9 salmon beads, 9 copper beads, 9 salmon beads.

Second tail section:

279 green beads, 9 salmon beads, 9 copper beads, 9 salmon beads.

Lower body increase:

String 160 green beads.

CROCHETING THE TAIL

1. Transfer the beads from the sewing thread to the crochet thread.

Row 1: Leaving a tail of about 18" (45 cm) of crochet thread to be used later for the copper loops, chain 9, putting a green bead in each chain stitch for the foundation row.

Row 2: Single bead crochet into the loop of the first bead in the chain to join the tube and continue crocheting 8 more beads around.

Rows 3–68: Continue working 9 beads around, ending with a salmon row. You have now completed the first and second tail sections.

CROCHETING THE LOWER BODY INCREASE

You will now increase a total of 8 beads over 12 rows. For a smoother look, the two increases in a row should be spread out evenly. Bead crochet as follows:

Row 1: Bead crochet 9 beads even.

Row 2: Bead crochet around, increasing 1 bead on beads 1 and 5 (11 beads total).

Rows 3–4: Bead crochet 11 beads even.

Row 5: Bead crochet around, increasing 1 bead on beads 3 and 9 (13 beads total).

Rows 6–7: Bead crochet 13 beads even.

Row 8: Bead crochet around, increasing 1 bead on beads 1 and 7 (15 beads total).

Rows 9–10: Bead crochet 15 beads even.

Row 11: Bead crochet around, increasing 1 bead on beads 4 and 12 (17 beads total).

Row 12: Bead crochet 17 beads even.

STRINGING THE LOWER BODY (MEDALLIONS)

1. String onto the sewing thread 1 row of 2 yellow beads and 15 green beads.
2. Starting at the top left, yellow bead of Chart 1, string onto the sewing thread Rows 1–32 of the chart 7 times for a total of 28 medallions.

HINT: Stringing and crocheting 6 medallions at a time will give you a manageable number of beads on your crochet thread.

3. At the same time, you will be increasing the number of yellow beads strung for the belly by a total of 2 beads. Rows 1–24 have 2 beads in the belly, Rows 25–64 have 3 beads, and all rows after that have 4 beads.

CROCHETING THE LOWER BODY

1. Transfer the beads from the sewing thread to the crochet thread.

Rows 1–225: Bead crochet a total of 28 medallions, stringing and crocheting 6 medallions at a time. Increase the belly beads as indicated in the stringing pattern.

STRINGING THE UPPER BODY (CHECKERBOARD PATTERN)

1. String onto the sewing thread 4 yellow beads, 1 green bead, 5 copper beads, 3 green beads, 5 copper beads, 1 green bead to complete the medallion pattern.
2. Starting with the top left yellow bead of Chart 2, string Rows 1–35.

CROCHETING THE UPPER BODY

1. Transfer the beads from the sewing thread to the crochet thread.

Rows 1–35: Bead crochet around.

STRINGING THE NECK AND TOP OF THE HEAD

1. Starting with the top left yellow bead of Chart 3, string onto the sewing thread Rows 1–28 of the chart. Continue to treat each row as one after the chart splits into two triangles. So in Row 14, string the 17 copper and green beads then the 15 salmon beads to count as 1 row.

NOTE: Because the mouth divides into two parts, the 2 groups of copper

```
 1  y y g c c c c c g g g g c c c c c g
 2  y y g c c c c g g g g g g c c c c g
 3  y y g c c c g g p p p p g g c c c g
 4  y y g c c g g p p p p p g g c c c g
 5  y y g c c g g p p b p p g g c c c g
 6  y y g c c g g p p p p p g g c c c g
 7  y y g c c c g g p p p g g c c c c g
 8  y y g c c c c g g g g g c c c c c g
 9  y y g c c c c c g g g c c c c c c g
10  y y g c c c c g g g g g c c c c c g
11  y y g c c c g g p p p g g c c c c g
12  y y g c c g g p p p p p g g c c c g
13  y y g c c g g p p b p p g g c c c g
14  y y g c c g g p p p p p g g c c c g
15  y y g c c c g g p p p g g c c c c g
16  y y g c c c c g g g g g c c c c c g
17  y y g c c c c c g g g c c c c c c g
18  y y g c c c c g g g g g c c c c c g
19  y y g c c c g g p p p g g c c c c g
20  y y g c c g g p p p p p g g c c c g
21  y y g c c g g p p b p p g g c c c g
22  y y g c c g g p p p p p g g c c c g
23  y y g c c c g g p p p g g c c c c g
24  y y g c c c c g g g g g c c c c c g
25  y y g c c c c c g g g c c c c c c g
26  y y g c c c c g g g g g c c c c c g
27  y y g c c c g g b b b g g c c c c g
28  y y g c c g g b b b b b g g c c c g
29  y y g c c g g b b p b b g g c c c g
30  y y g c c g g b b b b b g g c c c g
31  y y g c c c g g b b b g g c c c c g
32  y y g c c c c g g g g g c c c c c g
```

Belly Increases

row 1-24	2 yellow beads (as charted)
row 25-64	3 yellow beads (chart + 1 more)
row 65 on	4 yellow beads (chart + 2 more)

Color Legend

y = yellow

g = green

c = copper

p = purple

b = blue

Chart 1. Green Snake Lower Body. Repeat 7 times.

beads that look out of place in the chart are supposed to be there and the last two copper beads don't have a corresponding salmon row.

CROCHETING THE NECK

1. Transfer the beads from the sewing thread to the crochet thread.

Rows 1–11: Bead crochet around, increasing 1 yellow bead in every row. On odd-numbered rows, increase in the first bead of the yellow section. On even-numbered rows, increase in the last bead of the yellow section. You now have a tube consisting of 15 yellow beads and 15 green beads.

CROCHETING THE TOP OF THE HEAD

1. Using just thread and no beads, chain 15 and join with a slip stitch into the last yellow bead of the row on the opposite side of the neck. The thread chain should divide the tube in half

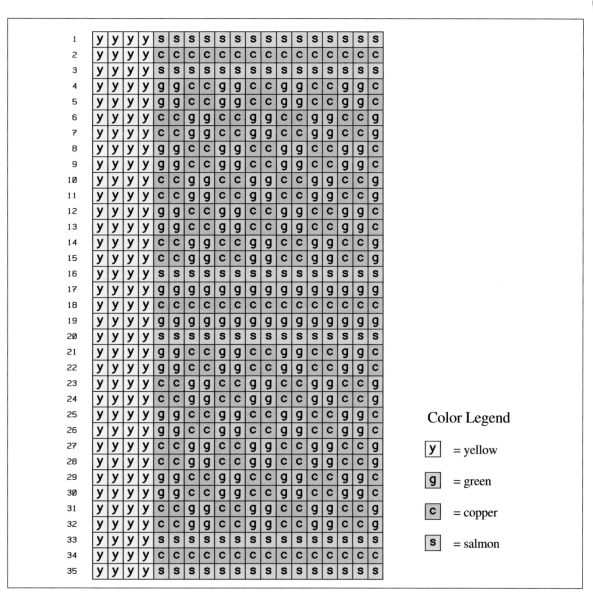

Color Legend

y = yellow

g = green

c = copper

s = salmon

Chart 2. Green Snake Upper Body.

with yellow beads on one side and green beads on the other. *See Figure 7.*

NOTE: This chain will serve as a foundation for the two halves of the mouth so don't worry if the chain appears to be too large; it will shrink as you crochet beads on both sides of it.

2. You should now be ready to crochet the green beads of Row 12 of the top of the snake's head, going around only the green beads and the new thread chain.

Row 12: Crochet both a copper bead and a green bead into that first green bead of the row. Continue to bead crochet to the last green bead in the row; crochet 1 green bead and 1 copper bead in that last green bead. Crochet the 15 salmon beads into the 15 thread chains. *See Figure 8.*

NOTE: The copper beads will form a

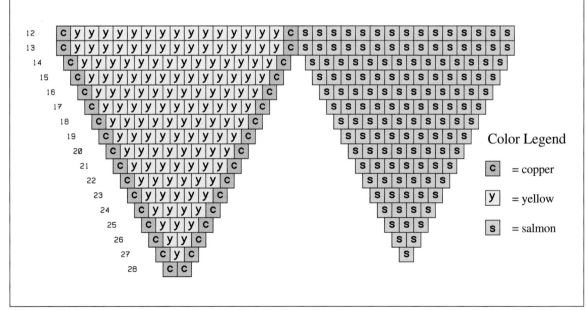

Chart 3. Green Snake Neck and Top of Head

Chart 4. Green Snake Bottom of Head

decorative ridge that divides the inside and outside of the mouth.

Row 13: Bead crochet around the green and salmon portions. *See Figure 9.*

Rows 14–27: Bead crochet around, decreasing 1 bead in the center of both the green and salmon portions of each row for a total decrease of 2 beads per row. As with the neck increases, the number of beads in every other row doesn't always divide exactly in half.

NOTE: The stringing chart cannot be used for the actual placement of the beads in the diamond motif while decreasing on the top of the head. It is easy enough, however, to determine by eye where the decrease comes in the diamond motif. On the bottom portion of the diamond, the copper beads will line up on top of the previous ones when you crochet them but the decrease in the middle of the diamond will result in the correct shape.

Row 28: Crochet the two copper beads with a slip stitch instead of the bead single crochet to help the beads form a tighter line. Leaving a 4" (10 cm) tail, cut the thread and fasten off.

STRINGING THE BOTTOM OF THE HEAD

1. Starting at the top left, copper bead of Chart 4, string the beads for Rows 12–28 according to the chart.

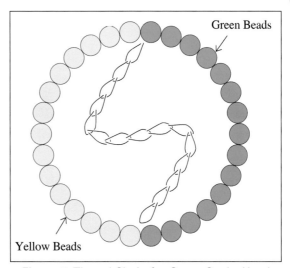

Figure 7. Thread Chain for Green Snake Head

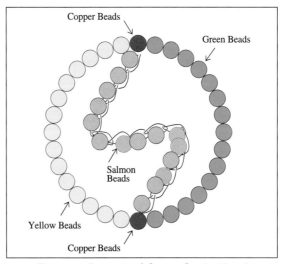

Figure 8. Row 12 of Green Snake Head

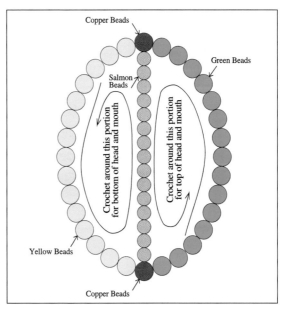

Figure 9. Row 12 completed.

CROCHETING THE BOTTOM OF THE HEAD

1. Transfer beads from the sewing thread to the crochet thread.

2. Fasten your crochet thread onto the loop of the first yellow bead of the mouth bottom using Steps 4–7 in Method 2 for joining a new thread. See the Techniques section.

Row 12: You are now ready to crochet the section of yellow beads. Crochet 1 copper and 1 yellow bead in the first yellow bead of the row. Bead crochet to the end of yellow portion, putting 1 yellow bead and 1 copper bead in the last yellow bead. Crochet the 15 salmon beads onto remaining loops of the added thread chain that now contains the first row of 15 salmon beads for the already completed mouth section.

Row 13: Bead crochet around the yellow and salmon portions

NOTE: The first few rows will be difficult to crochet but it will get easier as you get away from the junction of the two halves of the mouth.

Rows 14–27: Bead crochet around, decreasing 1 bead in both the yellow and salmon portions of the mouth for a total decrease of two beads per row. Decreases can be done in the middle of each section, as with the top of the head.

Row 28: Crochet the two copper beads using a slip stitch instead of a single crochet. Leaving a 4" (10 cm) tail, cut the thread and fasten off.

FINISHING THE MOUTH

1. If you don't want to wear the snake as a necklace, just pull both tail threads to the inside of the crochet. You can sew the mouth shut or leave it open.

2. If you want to use the snake as a necklace, you need to sew the mouth shut so that you can slip the tail through it. First, pull one of the thread tails to the inside of the crochet. To figure out where to sew the mouth closed, wrap the mouth around the tail right below where the body starts to increase, making sure that the mouth fits snugly around the tail. Mark that point with a straight pin or some other temporary marker. Take the tail out of the mouth and sew the mouth together at the mark (which will be about 3/8" or 1 cm from the tip) using one of the thread tails. Pull the other thread tail to the inside of the crochet.

TAIL LOOPS

1. Thread the reserved 18" (45 cm) of Cebelia thread from the start of the tail onto a needle and string 24 copper beads.

2. Taking your needle from the outside to the inside, go under the foundation thread loop of the next green bead and pull the thread through until the 24 beads form a loop. *See Figure 10.*

3. String another 24 copper beads and take the needle under the next foundation thread.

4. Continue around until there are 8 loops of 24 copper beads.

5. Knot off, cut remaining thread tail to about 3" (7.5 cm) and pull the remaining thread inside the tail.

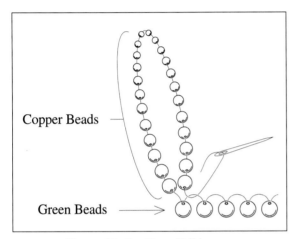

Figure 10. Necklace Tail Loops

Photo 51. Necklace Tail Loops

WEARING THE SNAKE AS A NECKLACE

Thread the tail through the mouth and arrange the snake around your neck. Photos 52 and 53 show two possible ways to wear a snake necklace.

Photo 52. One suggested necklace arrangement.

Photo 53. A second necklace arrangement.

Rattlesnake
Necklace

If the rattle on this snake seems a bit daunting, you can start with the matching bracelet. The technique is the same but the rattle is smaller.

MATERIALS

$1^1/_4$ hanks size 11° Czech yellow beads with red and blue stripes

½ hank size 11° Czech white with clear overlay beads

4 strands (from 1 hank) size 11° Czech shiny light brown beads

3 strands (from 1 hank) size 11° Czech shiny rose-pink beads

4 grams size 12° Japanese lavender beads (Matsuno 10M)

1 hank size 11° Czech opaque dark brown beads or 11 grams Asian beads (color 46, Hong Kong)

1 ball of gold DMC Cebelia size 30 cotton crochet thread (color 437)

1 spool sewing thread (any kind) for stringing

Polyester fiberfill or a cotton ball (optional)

TOOLS

1 size 10 (1.30 mm) or 11 (1.10 mm) steel crochet hook

Size 10 beading needles for stringing

Size 7 sharps sewing needles

GAUGE

12 beads around = 1" (2.5 cm)

12 rows = 1" (2.5 cm)

Measurement from start of rattle to last diamond on lower body (laid flat) = 25" (63.5 cm)

STRINGING THE BEADS FOR THE RATTLE AND THE TAIL:

1. String the following beads for the Rattle and Tail on to the sewing thread:

The Rattle:

60 light brown beads, 13 dark brown beads, 51 light brown beads, 13 dark brown beads, 92 light brown beads, 13 dark brown beads.

The Tail:

(150 yellow striped beads and 10 dark brown beads) 4 times.

CROCHETING THE RATTLE

You will be making 3 sections of light brown beads that increase and decrease within each section and are separated by a row of dark brown beads. Lightly stuff the rattle as you go along to help it keep its shape.

1. Transfer the beads from the sewing thread to the crochet thread. Bead crochet the first section as follows:

Row 1: Chain 7, putting 1 light brown bead in each chain (7 beads).

Row 2: Join chain with the first bead single crochet and continue to crochet 6 more beads around.

Row 3: Crochet 7 beads around.

Row 4: Increase 1 bead on beads 2, 4, and 6 (10 beads total).

Row 5: Increase 1 bead on beads # 3, 6, and 9 (13 beads total).

Row 6: Increase 1 bead on beads # 4, 8, and 12 (16 beads total).

Row 7: Decrease 1 bead on beads 5, 10, and 15 (13 dark brown beads total).

2. Bead crochet around the second section as follows:

Row 8: Increase 1 bead on beads 4, 8, and 12 (16 beads total).

Row 9: Increase 1 bead on beads 5, 10, and 15 (19 beads total).

Row 10: Decrease 1 bead on beads 6, 12, and 18 (16 beads total).

Row 11: Decrease 1 bead on beads 5, 10, and 15 (13 dark brown beads).

3. Bead crochet around for the third section as follows:

Row 12: Increase 1 bead on beads 4, 8, and 12 (16 beads total).

Row 13: Increase 1 bead on beads 5, 10, and 15 (19 beads total).

Row 14: Increase 1 bead on beads 6, 12, and 18 (22 beads total).

Row 15: Decrease 1 bead on beads 7, 14, and 21 (19 beads total).

Row 16: Decrease 1 bead on beads 6, 12, and 18 (16 beads total).

Row 17: Decrease 1 bead on beads 5, 10, and 15 (13 dark brown beads total).

CROCHETING THE TAIL

Row 1: Decrease 1 bead on beads 4, 8, and 12 (10 beads total).

Rows 2–64: Work even on 10 beads until you have 4 sections of 15 rows of striped beads with 1 row of dark brown beads.

STRINGING THE LOWER BODY INCREASE

1. String onto the sewing thread: 155 striped beads, 1 dark brown bead, 9 striped beads, 1 dark brown bead, and 2 striped beads.

HINT: Also string 2 diamonds of the Lower Body so that you have a decent number of beads to crochet.

STRINGING THE LOWER BODY (DIAMONDS)

1. Starting with the upper left white bead on Chart 5, string Rows 1–16 of the pattern 13 times for a total of 26 diamonds.

2. At the same time you will be increasing the number of white beads for the belly by a total of 2 beads. Rows 1–33 have 2 white beads, Rows 34–71 have 3 beads, and every row after that has 4 beads.

HINT: To work with the beads in manageable sections, string the first two diamonds with the Lower Body Increase then string 4 diamonds at a time.

CROCHETING LOWER BODY INCREASE

1. Transfer the beads from the sewing thread to the crochet thread.

Rows 1–2: Bead crochet 10 beads even.

Row 3: Increase 1 bead on beads 3 and 9 (12 beads total)

1	w	w	y	d	d	d	y	y	y	d	y	y	y	d	d	d	y
2	w	w	y	y	d	y	y	y	d	l	d	y	y	y	d	y	y
3	w	w	y	y	y	y	d	l	l	l	d	y	y	y	y		
4	w	w	y	y	y	y	d	l	l	r	l	l	d	y	y	y	y
5	w	w	y	y	y	d	l	l	r	r	r	l	l	d	y	y	y
6	w	w	y	y	y	y	d	l	l	r	l	l	d	y	y	y	y
7	w	w	y	y	y	y	y	d	l	l	d	y	y	y	y	y	y
8	w	w	y	y	d	y	y	y	d	l	d	y	y	y	d	y	y
9	w	w	y	d	d	d	y	y	y	d	y	y	y	d	d	d	y
10	w	w	y	y	d	y	y	y	d	p	d	y	y	y	d	y	y
11	w	w	y	y	y	y	d	p	p	p	d	y	y	y	y	y	
12	w	w	y	y	y	y	d	p	p	r	p	p	d	y	y	y	y
13	w	w	y	y	y	d	p	p	r	r	r	p	p	d	y	y	y
14	w	w	y	y	y	y	d	p	p	r	p	p	d	y	y	y	y
15	w	w	y	y	y	y	y	d	p	p	p	d	y	y	y	y	y
16	w	w	y	y	d	y	y	y	d	p	d	y	y	y	d	y	y

Belly Increases

row 1-33	2 white beads (as charted)
row 33-72	3 white beads (chart + 1 more)
row 73 on	4 white beads (chart + 2 more)

Color Legend

y = yellow striped

d = dark brown

l = light brown

r = rose pink

w = white

p = purple

Chart 5. Rattlesnake Lower Body. Repeat 13 times.

Rows 4–5: Bead crochet 12 beads even.

Row 6: Increase 1 bead on beads 1 and 6 (14 beads total).

Rows 7–8: Bead crochet 14 beads even.

Row 9: Increase 1 bead on beads 4 and 11 (16 beads total).

Rows 10–11: Bead crochet 16 beads even.

Row 12: Increase 1 bead on bead 8 (17 beads total).

Row 13: Bead crochet the 2 striped, 1 dark brown, 9 striped, 1 dark brown, and 2 striped beads.

CROCHETING LOWER BODY (DIAMONDS)

Rows 1–208: Bead crochet a total of 26 diamonds, stringing and crocheting 4 diamonds at a time. Increase the belly beads according to the stringing pattern.

STRINGING THE UPPER BODY (DOUBLE LOZENGE)

1. Starting with the upper left white bead of Chart 6, string Rows 1–37 of the chart.

Row																						
1	w	w	w	w	y	d	d	d	y	y	y	d	y	y	y	d	d	d	y			
2	w	w	w	w	y	y	d	y	y	y	d	l	d	y	y	y	d	y	y			
3	w	w	w	w	y	y	d	y	y	d	l	l	l	d	y	y	d	y	y			
4	w	w	w	w	y	y	d	y	y	d	l	l	l	d	y	y	d	y	y			
5	w	w	w	w	y	y	d	y	y	d	l	l	l	d	y	y	d	y	y			
6	w	w	w	w	y	y	d	y	y	d	l	l	l	d	y	y	d	y	y			
7	w	w	w	w	y	y	d	y	y	d	l	l	l	l	d	y	y	d	y	y		
8	w	w	w	w	y	y	d	y	y	d	l	l	l	d	y	y	d	y	y			
9	w	w	w	w	y	y	d	y	y	d	l	l	l	d	y	y	d	y	y			
10	w	w	w	w	y	y	d	y	y	d	l	l	l	d	y	y	d	y	y			
11	w	w	w	w	y	y	d	y	y	d	l	l	l	d	y	y	d	y	y			
12	w	w	w	w	y	y	d	y	y	d	l	l	l	d	y	y	d	y	y			
13	w	w	w	w	y	y	d	y	y	d	l	l	l	d	y	y	d	y	y			
14	w	w	w	w	y	y	d	y	y	d	l	l	l	d	y	y	d	y	y			
15	w	w	w	w	y	y	d	y	y	d	l	l	l	d	y	y	d	y	y			
16	w	w	w	w	y	y	d	y	y	d	l	l	l	d	y	y	d	y	y			
17	w	w	w	w	y	y	d	y	y	d	l	l	l	d	y	y	d	y	y			
18	w	w	w	w	y	y	d	y	y	y	d	l	d	y	y	y	d	y	y			
19	w	w	w	w	y	y	d	y	y	y	y	d	y	y	y	y	d	y	y			
20	w	w	w	w	y	y	d	y	y	y	d	l	d	y	y	y	d	y	y			
21	w	w	w	w	y	y	d	y	y	d	l	l	l	d	y	y	d	y	y			
22	w	w	w	w	y	y	d	y	y	d	l	l	l	d	y	y	d	y	y			
23	w	w	w	w	y	y	d	y	y	d	l	l	l	d	y	y	d	y	y			
24	w	w	w	w	y	y	d	y	y	d	l	l	l	d	y	y	d	y	y			
25	w	w	w	w	y	y	d	y	y	d	l	l	l	d	y	y	d	y	y			
26	w	w	w	w	y	y	d	y	y	d	l	l	l	d	y	y	d	y	y			
27	w	w	w	w	y	y	d	y	y	d	l	l	l	d	y	y	d	y	y			
28	w	w	w	w	y	y	d	y	y	d	l	l	l	d	y	y	d	y	y			
29	w	w	w	w	y	y	d	y	y	d	l	l	l	d	y	y	d	y	y			
30	w	w	w	w	y	y	d	y	y	d	l	l	l	d	y	y	d	y	y			
31	w	w	w	w	y	y	d	y	y	d	l	l	l	d	y	y	d	y	y			
32	w	w	w	w	y	y	d	y	y	d	l	l	l	d	y	y	d	y	y			
33	w	w	w	w	y	y	d	y	y	d	l	l	l	d	y	y	d	y	y			
34	w	w	w	w	y	y	d	y	y	d	l	l	l	d	y	y	d	y	y			
35	w	w	w	w	y	y	d	y	y	d	l	l	l	d	y	y	d	y	y			
36	w	w	w	w	y	y	d	y	y	y	d	l	d	y	y	y	d	y	y			
37	w	w	w	w	y	y	d	y	y	y	y	d	y	y	y	y	d	y	y			

Color Legend

y = yellow striped

d = dark brown

l = light brown

w = white

Chart 6. Rattlesnake Upper Body.

CROCHETING THE UPPER BODY (DOUBLE LOZENGE)

1. Transfer the beads from the sewing thread to the crochet thread.

Rows 1–37: Bead crochet around.

STRINGING THE NECK AND TOP OF THE HEAD

1. Starting with the top left white bead of Chart 7, string Rows 1–28 of the chart. Continue to treat each row as one after the chart splits into two triangles; so in Row 14, you string the 17 dark brown and striped beads then the 15 light brown beads to count as 1 row.

NOTE: Because the mouth divides into two parts, the 2 groups of 3 dark brown beads that look out of place in Row 12 of the chart are supposed to

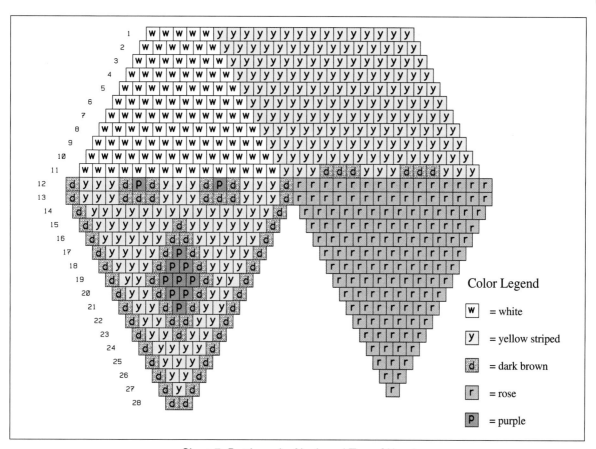

Chart 7. Rattlesnake Neck and Top of Head

be there and the last two dark brown beads don't have a corresponding light brown row.

CROCHETING THE NECK

1. Transfer the beads from the sewing thread to the crochet thread.

Rows 1–11: Bead crochet around, increasing 1 white bead in every row. On odd-numbered rows, increase in the first bead of the white section. On even-numbered rows, increase in the last bead of the white section. You now have a tube consisting of 15 white beads and 15 yellow striped beads.

CROCHETING THE TOP OF THE HEAD

1. Using just thread and no beads, chain 15 and join with a slip stitch into the last white bead in the row on the opposite side of the neck. The thread chain should divide the tube in half with white beads on one side and yellow striped beads on the other. *See Figure 11.*

NOTE: This chain will serve as a foundation for the two halves of the mouth, so don't worry if the chain appears to be too large; it will shrink as you crochet beads on both side of the chain.

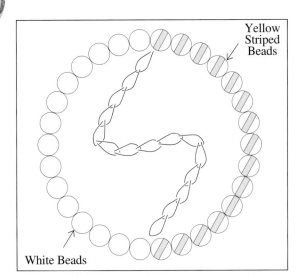

Figure 11. Thread chain for Rattlesnake Head

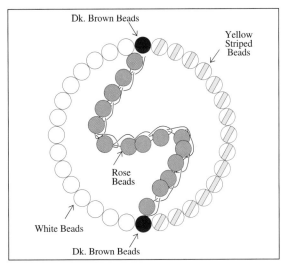

Figure 12. Row 12 of Rattlesnake Head

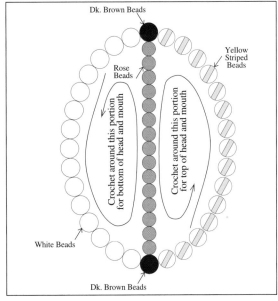

Figure 13. Row 12 completed.

2. You should now be ready to crochet the yellow striped beads in Row 12 of the top of the snake's head, going around only the yellow striped beads and the new thread chain.

Row 12: Crochet both a dark brown and a yellow striped bead into the first striped bead of the row. Continue to bead crochet to the last striped bead in the row; crochet 1 striped bead and 1 dark brown bead in that last yellow striped bead. Crochet the 15 rose beads into the 15 thread chains. *See Figure 12.*

NOTE: The dark brown beads will form a ridge that divides the inside and outside of the mouth.

Row 13: Bead crochet around the yellow striped and rose portions. *See Figure 13.*

Rows 14–27: Bead crochet around, decreasing 1 bead in the center of both the yellow striped and rose portions of each row for a total decrease of 2 beads per row.

NOTE: The stringing chart can not be used for the actual placement of the beads in the diamond motif while decreasing on the top of the head. It is easy enough, however, to determine by eye where the decreases should be in the diamond motif. On the bottom half of the diamond, the dark brown beads will line up one on top of the previous ones when you crochet them but the decrease in the middle of the diamond will result in the correct shape.

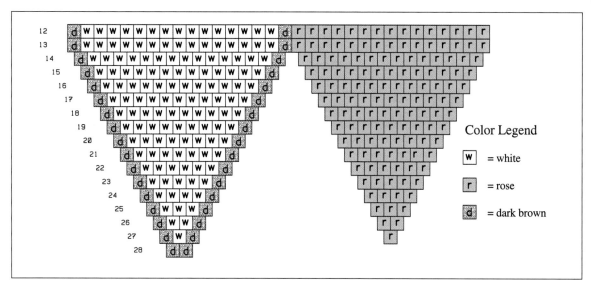

Chart 8. Rattlesnake Bottom of Head

Row 28: Crochet the two dark brown beads with a slip stitch instead of the bead single crochet to help the beads form a tighter line. Leaving a 4" (10 cm) tail, cut the thread and fasten off.

STRINGING THE BOTTOM OF THE HEAD

1. Starting at the top white bead on Chart 8, string Rows 12–28 according to the chart.

CROCHETING THE BOTTOM OF THE HEAD

1. Transfer the beads from the sewing thread to the crochet thread.

Row 12: Fasten the thread onto the loop of the first white bead of the mouth bottom so that you are ready to crochet the section of white beads. Crochet 1 dark brown and 1 white bead in the first white bead of the row. Bead crochet to the last white bead; crochet 1 white bead and 1 dark brown bead into the last white bead. Bead crochet the 15 rose beads onto the remaining loops of the added thread chain that now contains the first row of 15 rose beads for the already completed mouth section.

Row 13: Bead crochet around the white and rose portions.

NOTE: The first few rows will be difficult to crochet but it will get easier as you get away from the junction of the two halves of the mouth.

Rows 14–27: Bead crochet around, decreasing 1 bead in the middle of both the white and rose portions of the mouth for a total decrease of two beads per row.

Row 28: Crochet the two dark brown beads using a slip stitch instead of a single crochet to help the beads form a tighter line. Leaving a 4" (10 cm) tail, cut the thread and fasten off.

FINISHING THE MOUTH

1. If you don't want to wear the snake as a necklace, just pull both thread tails to the inside of the crochet. You can sew the mouth shut or leave it open.

2. If you want to wear the snake as a necklace, you need to sew the mouth shut. First pull one of the thread tails to the inside of the crochet. Then wrap the mouth around the tail right below where the body starts to increase. Pinch the tips of the mouth together towards the back until the mouth fits snugly around the tail. Mark that point with a straight pin or some other temporary marker. Take the tail out of the mouth and, using the remaining thread tail, sew the top and bottom of the mouth together at the mark (which will be about 3/8" or 1 cm from the tip). If you haven't done so, pull the thread tail from the beginning of the rattle to the inside of the snake.

WEARING THE SNAKE AS A NECKLACE

See the section on wearing the green snake as a necklace for two ways to wear the snake.

Rattlesnake
Bracelet

This adjustable bracelet will fit a wrist up to 8" (20 cm) around. The mouth is done a little differently from the longer snake necklaces in that there is thread crochet with no beads on the inside. If the rattle proves too daunting a start, make the snake without it. Then you can fasten on the thread at the tail and crochet the rattle after you have made the rest of the snake. See alternate instructions at the end.

MATERIALS

3 strands (from 1 hank or 5 grams) size 11° Czech yellow beads with red and blue stripes

1 strand (or 2 grams) size 11° Czech white core with clear overlay beads

1 strand (or 2 grams) size 11° Czech shiny light brown beads

1 strand (or 2 grams) size 12° Czech shiny rose-pink beads

1 gram size 12° Japanese matte lavender beads (Matsuno 10M)

2 grams size 11° matte dark brown beads (color 46, made in Hong Kong)

1 ball gold DMC Cebelia size 30 cotton crochet thread (color 437)

1 small piece of gold or tan felt

1 spool gold sewing thread

Small amount of polyester fiberfill or a cotton ball

1 size 00 snap

TOOLS

1 size 10 (1.30 mm) or 11 (1.10 mm) steel crochet hook

Size 10 beading needles for stringing

Size 7 sharps sewing needles

GAUGE

12 rows = 1" (2.5 cm)

STRINGING THE ENTIRE SNAKE:

1. String all of the following sections on to the sewing thread at one time:

The Rattle:

72 light brown beads, 5 dark brown beads.

The Tail:

1 white bead, 4 striped beads (27 times), 1 white bead, 5 striped beads (11 times).

The Body:

Starting at the top left white bead of Chart 9A, string Rows 1–49 of the chart.

The Neck and Top of the Head:

Starting at the top left white bead of Chart 10A, string Rows 1–15 of the chart.

The Bottom of the Head:

Starting at the top left dark brown bead of Chart 11A, string Rows 1–10 of the chart.

CROCHETING THE RATTLE

1. Transfer the beads from the sewing thread to the crochet thread.

Row 1: Chain 6, putting 1 light brown bead in each chain.

Row 2: Join chain with the first bead single crochet and continue to crochet 5 more beads around.

Row 3: Bead crochet around, increasing 1 bead on beads 3 and 6 (8 beads total).

Row 4: Increase 1 bead on beads 2, 4, 6, and 8 (12 beads total).

Row 5: Increase 1 bead on beads 6 and 12 (14 beads total).

Row	Cells (left → right)
1	w y y d y y
2	w y d l d y
3	w y y d y y
4	w y y y y y
5	w y y d y y
6	w y d p d y
7	w y y d y y
8	w y y y y y
9	w y y d y y
10	w y d l d y
11	w y y d y y
12	w y y y y y
13	w w y y d y y
14	w w y d p d y
15	w w y y d y y
16	w w y y y y y
17	w w y y d y y
18	w w y d l d y
19	w w y y d y y
20	w w y y y y y
21	w w y y d y y
22	w w y d p d y
23	w w w y y d y y
24	w w w y y y y y
25	w w w y y d y y
26	w w w y d l d y
27	w w w y y d y y
28	w w w y y y y y
29	w w w y y d y y
30	w w w y d p d y
31	w w w y y d y y
32	w w w y y y y y
33	w w w w y y d y y
34	w w w w y d l d y
35	w w w w y y d y y
36	w w w w y y y y y
37	w w w w y y d y y
38	w w w w y d p d y
39	w w w w y y d y y
40	w w w w y y y y y
41	w w w w y y d y y
42	w w w w y d l d y
43	w w w w w y y d y y
44	w w w w w y y y y y
45	w w w w w y y d y y
46	w w w w w y d p d y
47	w w w w w y y d y y
48	w w w w w y y y y y
49	w w w w w d d d d d

Color Legend

y = yellow striped

d = dark brown

l = light brown

p = purple

w = white

Chart 9A. Rattlesnake Bracelet

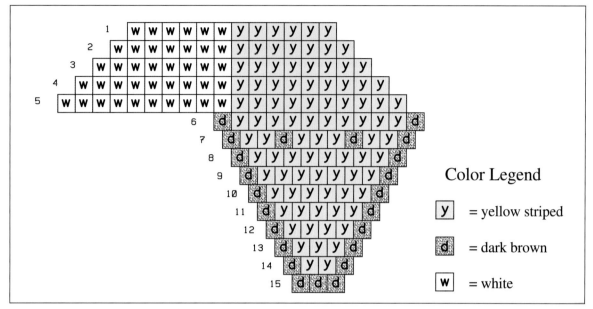

Chart 10A. Rattlesnake Neck and Top of Head

Row 6: Decrease 1 bead on beads 7 and 13 (12 beads total).

Row 7: Decrease 1 bead on beads 3, 6, 9, and 11 (8 beads total). With your crochet hook, pull the beginning thread tail to the inside of the rattle and use it to stuff the rattle. If you need more support in the rattle, add a small piece of fiberfill or cotton.

Row 8: Decrease 1 bead on bead 2 and 6 (6 beads total).

Row 9: Decrease 1 bead on bead 3 (5 dark brown beads total).

CROCHETING THE TAIL

Rows 1–27: Bead crochet around on 5 beads.

Row 28: Increase 1 bead on bead 3 (6 beads total).

Rows 29–38: Bead crochet around on 6 beads.

CROCHETING THE BODY

Rows 1-37: Bead crochet around, increasing white beads according to the stringing pattern. Increases should be placed in the last striped bead before the white section in each row.

CROCHETING THE NECK

Rows 1–5: Bead crochet around, increasing 1 bead in the first bead of both the white and striped sections. You will now have 20 beads around.

CROCHETING THE TOP OF THE HEAD

1. Using just thread and no beads, chain 10 and join with a slip stitch to last white bead in the row on the opposite side of the neck. The thread chain should divide the tube in half with white beads on one side and yellow

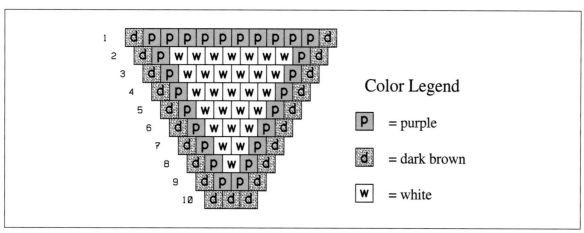

Chart 11A. Rattlesnake Bottom of the Head.

Color Legend

p	= purple
d	= dark brown
w	= white

striped beads on the other. *See Figure 14.*

2. You should now be ready to crochet the yellow striped beads of Row 6 of the top of the snake's head, going around only the striped section and the new thread chain. *See Figure 15.*

Row 6: Crochet both a dark brown bead and a striped bead into the first striped bead. Continue to bead crochet to the last striped bead in the row; crochet 1 striped bead and 1 dark brown bead in that last striped bead. Without using beads, do 10 single crochets in the 10 chains of the new thread chain.

NOTE: The dark brown beads will form a ridge that divides the inside and outside of the mouth.

Rows 7–14: Work around, doing bead single crochet on the outside striped portion and plain single crochet on the inside of the mouth. At the same time, decrease 1 bead in the middle of the striped bead section and 1 stitch

in the inside plain section on every row.

Row 15: Skipping the next dark brown bead, crochet the 3 dark brown beads using a slip stitch instead of a single crochet. Leaving a 3" (7.5 cm) tail, cut the thread and fasten off.

PREPARING THE FELT INTERLINING FOR THE MOUTH

The felt interlining goes on the inside of the snake to provide support for the snap. You will not see it when the mouth is finished.

1. Place the finished Top of the Head on the felt and trace around the head with a pencil to make a pattern. Remove the snake and draw a horizontal line across the bottom of the mouth to indicate the fold.

2. Fold the felt in half along the bottom of the mouth and cut out the two layers on the pencil line so that you have an oval shape.

3. Trim the oval shape until it can fit easily inside the top of the mouth between the outside bead portion and inside plain crochet portion. Place half of the felt piece inside the crochet.

4) You are now ready to finish the Bottom of the Head, crocheting around the second half of the felt piece.

HINT: If the felt interlining gets in the way as you crochet around it, fasten the felt out of the way with a straight pin.

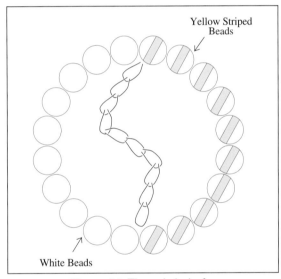

Figure 14. Thread chain for Rattlesnake Bracelet Head.

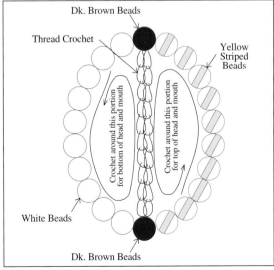

Figure 15. Row 6 completed.

CROCHETING THE BOTTOM OF THE HEAD

Row 1: Fasten your thread onto the loop for the first white bead in the row and crochet 1 dark brown bead and 1 white bead into that same white bead. Bead crochet to the last white bead; crochet 1 white bead and 1 dark brown bead in that last white bead. Without using beads, do 10 single crochets on the free loops of the added thread chain that now contains the first row of 10 plain crochet stitches for the top of the head.

Rows 2–9: Work around, doing bead single crochet on the outside white beaded portion and plain single crochet on the inside of the mouth. At the same time, decrease 1 bead in the middle of the beaded portion and 1 stitch in the plain portion of the mouth on every row.

Row 10: Bead crochet the last 3 dark brown beads using a slip stitch instead of a single crochet. Leaving a 3" (7.5 cm) tail, cut the thread and fasten off.

FINISHING THE SNAKE

1. Pull the 2 mouth thread tails to the inside of the crochet.

2. Place the female portion of the snap as close to the front of the bottom of the mouth as possible while still leaving enough room to sew the snap on. Using sewing thread, stitch the female portion of the snap to the bottom of

the mouth, making sure to go through the felt interlining.

3. Place the male portion of the snap on the top of the mouth to match the placement of the female portion and sew in place, again stitching through the felt.

ALTERNATIVE RATTLE
CROCHETING THE RATTLE
AT THE END

Stringing the Rattle

Onto the sewing thread, string 5 dark brown beads and 71 light brown beads.

Crocheting the Rattle

1. Transfer beads from sewing thread to crochet thread.

Row 1: Fasten thread on 1 of the thread loops of the original foundation chain. Bead single crochet 5 dark brown beads in the 5 foundation loops.

Row 2: Bead crochet around, increasing 1 bead on bead #3 (6 beads total).

Row 3: Increase 1 bead on beads #2 and 4 (8 beads total).

Row 4: Increase 1 bead on beads 1, 3, 5, and 7 (12 beads total).

Row 5: Increase 1 on beads 1 and 7 (14 beads total).

Row 6: Decrease 1 bead on bead 4 and 8 (12 beads total). Put a bit of stuffing in the rattle.

Row 7: Decrease 1 bead on beads 1, 4, 7, and 10 (8 beads total).

Row 8: Decrease 1 bead on beads 3 and 7 (6 beads total).

Row 9: Decrease 1 bead on bead 1 (5 beads total). Cut the thread, fasten off, and pull the thread to the inside of the snake.

WEARING THE SNAKE
AS A BRACELET

1. Wrap the snake around your wrist.

2. Put the snake's tail through the open mouth to form a circle and fasten the snap.

3. If the extra tail section is long enough, you can tuck it underneath the snake's head.

Green Snake Bracelet

MATERIALS

5 grams size 12° Japanese green seed beads (Matsuno 22FAB)

1 strand (or 2 grams) size 11° Czech yellow seed beads (or size 12° Matsuno 1)

1 gram size 12° Japanese copper seed beads (Matsuno 176)

1 gram size 12° Japanese purple seed beads (Matsuno 13/207)

1 gram size 12° Japanese salmon seed beads (Matsuno 9F)

1 gram size 10° or 11° Czech light blue seed beads

1 ball green DMC Cebelia size 30 cotton crochet thread (color 955)

1 spool green sewing thread to match crochet thread

1 small piece green felt

1 size 00 snap

TOOLS

1 size 10 (1.30 mm) or 11 (1.10 mm) steel crochet hook

Size 10 beading needles for stringing

Size 7 sharps sewing needles

GAUGE

12 rows= 1" (2.5 cm)

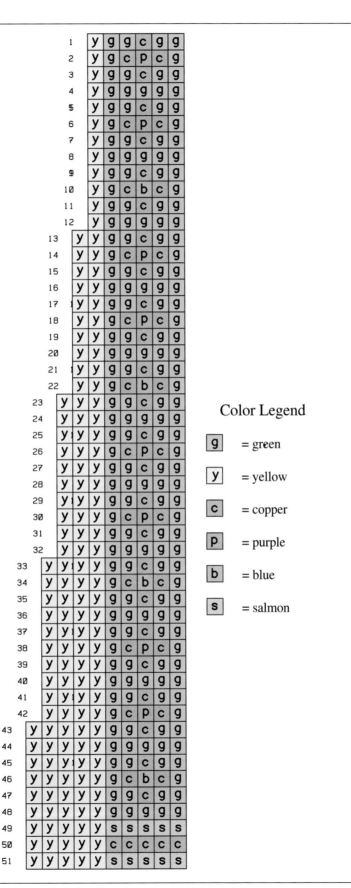

Chart 9B. Green Snake Bracelet

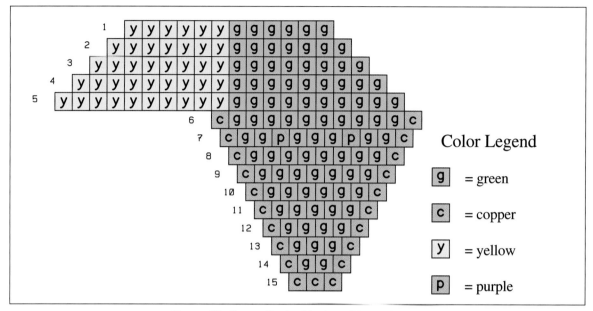

Chart 10B. Green Snake Neck and Top of Head

STRINGING THE ENTIRE SNAKE:

1. String all of the following sections on to the sewing thread at one time:

The Tail:

(1 yellow bead, 4 green beads) 27 times.

(1 yellow, 5 green beads) 11 times.

The Body:

Starting at the top left yellow bead of Chart 9B, string Rows 1–51 of the chart.

The Neck and Top of the Head:

Starting at the top left yellow bead of Chart 10B, string Rows 1–15 of the chart.

The Bottom of the Head:

Starting at the top left copper bead of Chart 11B, string Rows 1–10 of the chart.

CROCHETING THE TAIL

1. Transfer beads from the sewing thread to the crochet thread.

Row 1: Leaving a 16" (40.5 cm) tail of thread to be used for the tail loops, chain 5 while putting 1 bead in each chain.

Row 2: Join chain with the first bead single crochet, bead crochet 4 more beads.

Rows 3–27: Bead crochet around on 5 beads.

Row 28: Increase 1 bead on bead 3 (6 beads total).

Rows 29–38: Bead crochet around on 6 beads.

CROCHETING THE BODY

Rows 1–37: Bead crochet around, increasing yellow beads according to the stringing pattern. Increases should

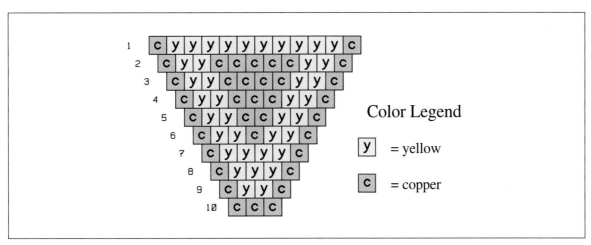

Chart 11B. Green Snake Bottom of the Head.

be placed in the last green bead before the yellow section in each row.

CROCHETING THE NECK

Rows 1–5: Bead crochet around, increasing 1 bead in the first bead of both the yellow and green sections. You will now have 20 beads around.

CROCHETING THE TOP OF THE HEAD

1. Using just thread and no beads, chain 10 and join with a slip stitch to last yellow bead in the row on the opposite side of the neck. The thread chain should divide the tube in half with yellow beads on one side and green beads on the other. *See Figure 14 of the Rattlesnake Bracelet.*

2. You should now be ready to crochet the green beads of Row 6 of the top of the snake's head, going around only the green section and the new thread chain. *See Figure 15.*

Row 6: Crochet both a copper bead and a green bead into the first green bead. Continue to bead crochet to the last green bead in the row; crochet 1 green bead and 1 copper bead in that last green bead. Without using beads, do 10 single crochets in the 10 chains of the new thread chain.

NOTE: The copper beads will form a ridge that divides the inside and outside of the mouth.

Rows 7–14: Work around, doing bead single crochet on the outside green portion and plain single crochet on the inside of the mouth. At the same time, decrease 1 bead in the middle of the green bead section and 1 stitch in the inside plain section on every row.

Row 15: Skipping the next copper bead, bead crochet the 3 copper beads using a slip stitch instead of a single crochet. Leaving a 3" (7.5 cm) tail, cut the thread and fasten off.

PREPARING THE FELT INTERLINING FOR THE MOUTH

The felt interlining goes on the inside of the snake to provide support for the snap. You will not see it when the mouth is finished.

1. Place the finished Top of the Head on the felt and trace around the head with a pencil to make a pattern. Remove the snake and draw a horizontal line across the bottom of the mouth to indicate the fold.
2. Fold the felt in half along the bottom of the mouth and cut out the two layers on the pencil line so that you have an oval shape.
3. Trim the oval shape until it can fit easily inside the top of the mouth between the outside bead portion and inside plain crochet portion. Place half of the felt piece inside the crochet.
4. You are now ready to finish the bottom of the head, crocheting around the second half of the felt lining.

HINT: If the felt interlining gets in the way as you crochet around it, fasten the felt out of the way with a straight pin.

CROCHETING THE BOTTOM OF THE HEAD

Row 1: Fasten your thread onto the loop for the first yellow bead in the row and crochet 1 copper bead and 1 yellow bead into that same yellow bead. Bead crochet to the last yellow bead; crochet 1 yellow bead and 1 copper bead in that last yellow bead. Without using beads, do 10 single crochets in the 10 free loops of the added thread chain that now contains the first row of 10 plain crochet stitches for the top of the head.

Rows 2–9: Work around, doing bead single crochet on the outside yellow beaded portion and plain single crochet on the inside of the mouth. At the same time, decrease 1 bead in the middle of the beaded portion and 1 stitch in the plain portion of the mouth on every row.

Row 10: Skipping the next copper bead, crochet the last 3 copper beads using a slip stitch instead of a single crochet. Leaving a 3" (7.5 cm) tail, cut the thread and fasten off.

TAIL LOOPS

1. Thread the 16" (40.5 cm) tail of crochet thread from the beginning of the snake onto either a beading needle or a sewing needle. Use whatever size needle will allow you to go through the beads twice.
2. String 1 copper bead, 1 salmon bead, 7 copper beads, 1 salmon bead, and 7 copper beads on your crochet thread.
3. Pass the needle back through the first salmon and copper beads next to the bead crochet tail and pull up the excess thread to make the first loop. *See Figure 16.*

4. Move to the next location by passing the needle underneath the next thread loop of the bead crochet foundation and pulling the thread through.

5. Repeat Steps 2-4 until you have a total of 5 loops around the tail.

6. Knot off. Pull the 3" thread tail to the inside of the snake.

FINISHING THE SNAKE

1. Pull the 2 thread tails from the mouth to the inside of the crochet.

2. Place the female portion of the snap as close to the front of the bottom mouth as possible while still leaving enough room to sew on the snap. Using sewing thread, stitch the female portion of the snap to the bottom of the mouth, making sure to go through the felt interlining.

3. Place the male portion of the snap on the top of the mouth to match the placement of the female portion and sew in place, again stitching through the felt.

WEARING THE SNAKE AS A BRACELET

1. Wrap the snake around your wrist.

2. Put the snake's tail through the open mouth to form a circle and fasten the snap.

3. If the extra tail section is long enough, you can tuck it underneath the snake's head.

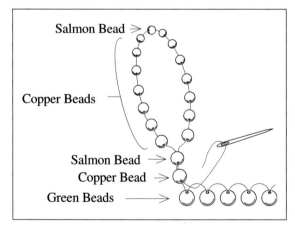

Figure 16. Bracelet Tail Loops.

Photo 54

Photo 55. Additional supplies and tools for
the Memory Wire Snake Bracelet.

Pictured is the 2¹/4" bracelet memory wire and special
F-C3 Felco wire cutters for the memory wire. Do not use
regular wire cutters or you will damage the tool. You may
also use a rotary tool, such as those made by Dremel, to cut
the memory wire.

Memory Wire
Snake Bracelet

This design is a bit different because it employs a stringing pattern that alternates between an even and uneven number of beads in each row. When you crochet the snake bracelet, the number of beads in a row remains the same and the beadwork still spirals, but the flowers appear to sit in a straight line.

MATERIALS

10 grams size 12° Japanese red seed beads (Matsuno color 736)

6 grams size 12° Japanese white core with amber overlay seed beads (Matsuno color 1/212)

4 grams size 12° Japanese black seed beads (Matsuno color 748)

3 grams size 12° Japanese metallic gold seed beads (Matsuno color 561)

1 ball red DMC Cebelia size 30 cotton crochet thread

Sewing thread of any color for stringing

2$\frac{1}{2}$ rounds (about 16" or 40.5 cm) of 2$\frac{1}{4}$" bracelet memory wire .024

TOOLS

1 size 10 (1.30 mm) or 11 (1.10 mm) steel crochet hook

Size 10 beading needles for stringing

Size 7 sharps sewing needles, optional

Wire cutters for memory wire

GAUGE

12 rows = 1" (2.5 cm)

STRINGING THE TAIL AND BODY

1. On the sewing thread, string 36 red beads, then string 6 repeats of Chart 12, 4 repeats of Chart 13, 4 repeats of Chart 14, 4 repeats of Chart 15, and 4 repeats of Chart 16 for the rest of the body.

HINT: Since the snake is too long to string in one go, the most efficient way to do it is to string from the 36 red beads to the end of Chart 14 for the first group. String Chart 15 through Chart 17 for the second group.

STRINGING THE HEAD

1. Starting at the top left, black bead of Chart 17, string the beads according to the chart.

WORKING WITH THE MEMORY WIRE

You can either thread the memory wire through the snake as you crochet or you can thread the wire through after you have crocheted the snake up to the decrease portion of the head. If you thread the wire as you crochet make sure that the wire doesn't accidentally slip out the back as you are working.

HINT: If you add the wire after you have crocheted most of the snake, there is a little trick to getting the wire past the smaller section of the tail. Take a knitting needle or dowel that is the same size as the inside of the tail and push the beaded tail on to the knitting needle or dowel, scrunching up the tail a bit. This will temporarily make the inside of the tail wider. Remove the tail from the knitting needle or dowel and thread the memory wire through the tail.

When cutting the memory wire, use wire cutters specifically made to cut memory wire. Do not use scissors or regular wire cutters because you will damage them.

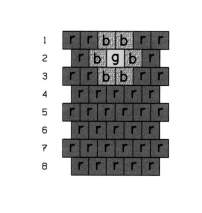

Chart 12.
Memory Wire Snake Bracelet
Repeat 6 times

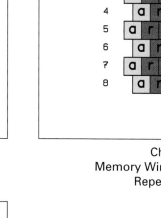

Chart 13.
Memory Wire Snake Bracelet
Repeat 4 times

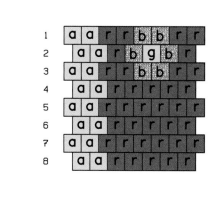

Chart 14.
Memory Wire Snake Bracelet
Repeat 4 times

Color Legend

r	= red
b	= black
g	= gold
a	= amber

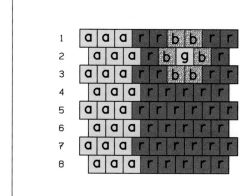

Chart 15.
Memory Wire Snake Bracelet
Repeat 4 times

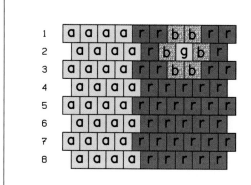

Chart 16.
Memory Wire Snake Bracelet
Repeat 4 times

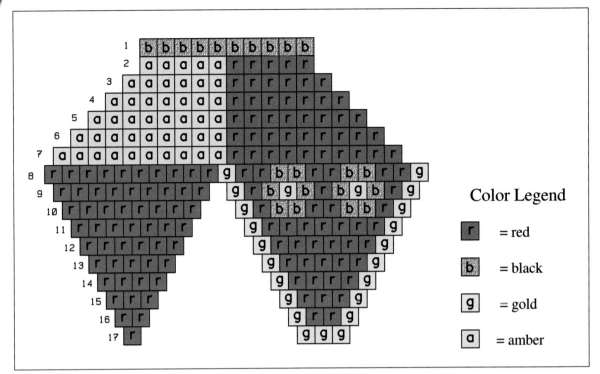

Chart 17. Memory Wire Snake Bracelet Head

CROCHETING THE TAIL AND BODY

1. Transfer the beads from the sewing thread to the crochet thread.

Row 1: Leaving an 11" (28 cm) tail of thread, chain 6, putting 1 bead in each chain.

Row 2: Single bead crochet into the loop of the first bead in the chain to form a tube and crochet another 5 beads in the remaining 5 loops.

Rows 3–54: Bead crochet around the 6-bead tube.

Row 55: Increase 1 bead by crocheting the amber belly bead in the same loop as the last red bead of row 54 (7 around). This row is the first row of Chart 13.

Rows 56–151: Continue bead crocheting around, increasing 1 amber bead according to the pattern. All amber bead increases are done in the red bead before the amber belly.

CROCHETING THE HEAD

Row 1: Bead crochet the 10 black beads.

Row 2: Bead crochet the 5 amber beads and the 5 red beads.

Rows 3–7: Bead crochet around, increasing 1 bead in the first bead of both the amber and red portions of the row until you have 10 amber beads and 10 red beads.

Row 8: Switching colors on the amber portion, bead crochet 10 red beads, crochet 1 red and 1 gold bead in the next stitch. Bead crochet to the end of the row, again increasing 1 gold bead on the last stitch. The added gold beads will form a line separating the top and bottom of the head.

Row 9: Crochet 5 red beads, decrease 1, crochet 3 red beads. Crochet 1 gold, 1 red, 1 black, 1 gold, 1 black bead. Decrease by skipping the next loop. Crochet to end of row.

Row 10: Crochet 4 red beads, decrease 1, crochet 3 red beads. Crochet 1 gold, 1 red, 2 black, 1 red bead. Decrease by skipping the next loop. Crochet 1 red, 2 black, 1 red, and 1 gold bead.

Row 11: Thread the memory wire through the snake. With pliers, bend a loop in the top end (at the head) that measures $3/16$" (.5 cm) across. Twist the loop sideways a bit so that it is parallel to the snake's head and won't poke through the beads at the bottom of the head. Bead crochet around, decreasing 1 stitch in the middle of the top and bottom portions of the head.

Rows 12–16: Bead crochet around, decreasing 1 bead in the middle of both the top and bottom of the head. Move the wire loop up as you crochet.

Row 17: Crochet 1 gold bead, decrease 1 red bead. Skip the next gold bead in the previous row and crochet the last 3 gold beads using a slip stitch. Fasten off, leaving an 8" (20 cm) tail of thread.

FINISHING THE HEAD

1. Thread a sewing needle with the 8" (20 cm) tail of crochet thread and close up the small hole in the tip of the nose with 1 or 2 stitches.

2. Push the memory wire loop as close to the tip of the nose as possible.

3. With the same thread and needle, sew wire loop in place with 2 stitches in 2 or 3 places along the memory wire loop.

4. Make sure the snake head angles down. If not, adjust the wire loop.

5. Knot the thread. Pull the excess few inches of the thread tail to the inside of the snake.

FINISHING THE TAIL

1. On the memory wire, mark the end of the tail with a piece of tape. Cut the memory wire at that mark.

2. Make a loop in the memory wire that is as small as possible, a little under $1/8$" (.3 cm). The loop must fit inside the crochet tube. If the loop is too big, cut the wire shorter and make another loop.

3. Thread a needle with the 11" (28 cm) thread tail. Arrange the pattern on the snake so that the flowers line up.

4. Sew through the thread loops on either side of the tail once to keep the memory wire inside. Then sew through the thread loops and the memory wire a few times to secure the beadwork to the wire loop. Knot thread but don't cut it.

5. To make gold loops, pick up 4 gold beads, 1 black bead, and 4 gold beads on your needle. Take the needle and thread under 1 of the foundation loops of the tail and pull thread through. Repeat up to 4 times.

6. Knot the thread. Pull the excess few inches of the thread tail to the inside of the snake.

BIBLIOGRAPHY

Blunt, Fanny Janet and Stanley Lane Poole (editor). *The people of Turkey: twenty years residence among Bulgarians, Greek, Albanians, Turks, and Armenians.* London: John Murray, 1878.

"British Treatment of enemy Prisoners," *Manx Quarterly #17* (October, 1916). *http://www.isle-of-man.com/manxnotebook/mquart/mq17071.htm*

Csukovits, Anita. "Art under pressure—Artifacts of Hungarian prisoners in the 19-20th century showed in the exhibition room of the Greek Tempel in Vac," *Neprajzi ertesito Annales Musei ethnographiae, 84 (2002): 145.*

Durham, M. E. *Some tribal origins, laws, and customs of the Balkans.* London: George Allen & Unwin Ltd., 1928.

Edwards, Holly. "Ex-Iraqi prisoner threaded beauty in midst of suffering," *Tennessean,* May 12, 2003. *http://www.tennessean.com.*

Emergency Committee for the Assistance of Germans, Austrians, and Hungarians in Distress. *Report.* London, 1914-1919.

Garnett, Lucy M. J. *Balkan home life.* London: Methuen & Co. Ltd., 1917.

Garnett, Lucy M. J., *The women of turkey and their folk-lore.* London: David Nutt, 1893.

Gjergji, Andromaqi. *Traditional Culture in Albania. http://www.seda.org/al/ACH/cult.htm*

Hawthorne, Lesleyanne. *Johnny Turk.* Melbourne, Australia: ATFS Publications, 1986. *http://www.atmg.org.*

Hiiemae, Mall. *Some Possible Origins of St. George's Day Customs and Beliefs. http://www.folklore.ee/folklore/nr1/georg.htm.*

Honey, Denise. "Christ behind bars." *WINnews: The quarterly newsletter of World In Need* (Winter 2006). *http://www.winint.org/FEB2006.pdf.*

Holmes, Burton. *Burton Holmes travelogues: with illustrations from photographs by the author.* New York: The McClure Co., 1910.

International Committee of the Red Cross. *Turkish Prisoners in Egypt.* London: Cassell & Co., 1917.

Kimball, Jane. *Trench Art: An Illustrated History.* Davis, California: Silverpenny Press, 2004.

"Knockaloe Relics Return to the Isle of Man-Manx National Heritage News Release." October 16, 2002. *http://www.gov.im/infocentre/archived_releases/PR_mnh_01/mnh_bones.html*

Krautwurst, Terry (editor). *500 Beaded Objects: New Dimensions in Contemporary Beadwork.* New York: Lark Books, 2004.

Lawrence, Robert Means. *The magic of the horse-shoe, with other folk-lore notes.* Detroit, Michigan: Singing Tree Press, 1968.

Lodge, Olive. "Folk Festivals in Yugoslavia," *Folklore, 55,* No. 2 (June 1944): 59-68.

Marischal Virtual Museum. "Margaret Hasluck." *http://www.abdn.ac.uk/virtualmuseum/index.php?page=caseview&display=27&roomlocations=sg_groundexhibition=LostRitual.*

Milgram, Miriam. *Balkan Beaded Crochet.* New York: Miriam Milgram, 1998.

Onuk, Taciser. *Oya Culture Since the Ottomans.* Trans. Barbara Blackwell Gülen. Akara, Turkey: T. C. Kultur Bakanligi, 2000.

Oprescu, George. *Peasant Art in Roumania.* London: The Studio, 1929.

Paludan, Lis. *Crochet: History & Technique.* Loveland, Colorado: Interweave Press, 1995.

Parker-Fairbanks, Dixie. *Silent sunflowers, a Balkan memoir: two American artists and their search for vanishing folk art.* Seattle, Washington: University of Washington Press, ca. 2000.

Parkinson, Maude Rea. *Twenty Years in Roumania.* London: George Allen & Unwin, Ltd., 1921.

Pye, Ernest. *Prisoner of War, 31,163, Bedros M. Sharian.* New York: Fleming H. Revell Company, 1938.

Quayle, Frank C. "Knockaloe Moar." *Isle of Man Family History Society Journal,* 12, No. 4 (Nov 1990). *http://www.isle-of-man.com/manxnotebook/famhist/v12n4.htm*

Raykova, Mariana. *Bulgarian folk costumes from Thrace.* Sofia, Bulgaria: Nikrima, 2003.

Sargeaunt, Bertram Edward. *The Isle of Man and the Great War.* Douglas, Isle of Man: Brown, 1920.

Saunders, Nicholas J. *Trench Art: Materialities and Memories of War.* Oxford and New York: Berg, 2003.

Thomas, Anna Braithwaite. *St. Stephen's House: Friends' Emergency Work in England 1914–1920.* London: Emergency Committee for the Assistance of Germans, Austrians, and Hungarians in Distress, ca. 1920.

Tomalin, Stefany. "Crocheted Snakes." *Bead Society of Great Britain Newsletter,* No. 30.

Ugurlu, Aydin. "Creatures of Imagination." *Skylife: Turkish Airlines Magazine. (*March, 2002). *http://www.thy.com/en-INT/skylife/archive/en/2002_3/konu6.htm#1.*

United States, Dept. of State. *Reports of visits of inspection made by officials of the United States embassy to various internment camps in the United Kingdom.* London: Harrison and Sons, 1916.

Right: Two bead crochet snakes made by Yoshie Marubashi, measuring 34″ (86.5 cm) and 36″ (91.5 cm).

Below: Me and My Shadow: Color Study, Adele Rogers Recklies, 2003. Each snake measures 32″ (81 cm) long.

INDEX

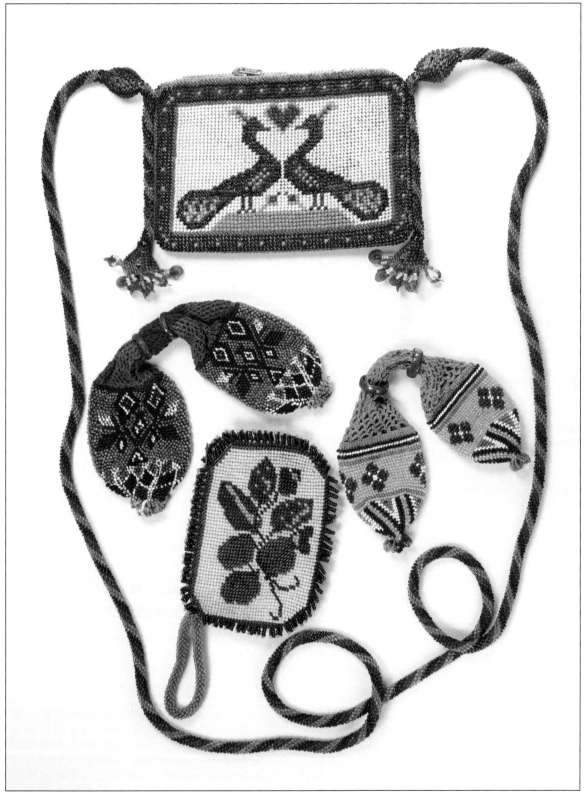

Four bead crochet purses from Turkey and Bulgaria. *Top,* small bag with zipper and leather lining measuring 6³/₄″ (17 cm) x 4¹/₄″ (11 cm); *middle,* two misers purses, the largest measuring 9¹/₂″ (24 cm) x 2¹/₄″ (5.5 cm); *bottom,* coin purse with zipper and cloth lining, measuring 4³/₄″ (12 cm) x 3¹/₂″ (9 cm).

Another view of *Why Is Everybody Always Picking on Me?* that shows more of the common negative sayings about snakes. Photo by D. James Dee.

ABOUT THE AUTHOR

Adele Rogers Recklies, has had a career that encompasses both beads and fiber, academic work and creative play. Before working as a costume maker for professional theater, she earned a B.A. and M.A. from Kent State University and a Ph.D. in theater from The Ohio State University. After teaching in a small college and working for two different costume shops in New York City, Dr. Recklies opened her own business in 1987 to specialize in theatrical knitting, crochet, and related crafts.

Dr. Recklies' embroidery work can be seen in the recent movie *Memoirs of a Geisha*. Her knitted costumes have been worn in other movies such as *Lemony Snicket's A Series of Unfortunate Events, Charlie's Angels: Full Throttle, Big Fish,* and *Stepmom* as well as Broadway shows such as *CATS*. Some of her beadwork was included in *500 Beaded Objects: New Dimensions in Contemporary Beadwork* and exhibited at Bead International 2006 at The Dairy Barn Arts Center as well as the Masami Sato & Members of The Bead Society of Greater New York shows at the Nihonbashi Takashimaya, Tokyo, Japan in 2003 and 2004.